SOMETHIN' OUTTA NOTHIN'

LORENZO ESPADA

SOMETHIN' OUTTA NOTHIN'

LORENZO ESPADA

DK | Penguin Random House

Publisher Mike Sanders
Senior Editor Olivia Peluso
Art & Design Director William Thomas
Designer Lindsay Dobbs
Recipe Photographer Jonathan Cooper
Lifestyle Photographer Will "SimplisticPhobia" Jenkins
Food Stylist Ashley Johnson
Recipe Tester Diamond Alexander
Proofreaders Bill Bowers & Claire Safran
Indexer Celia McCoy

First American Edition, 2023
Published in the United States by DK Publishing
1745 Broadway, 20th Floor, New York, NY 10019

The authorized representative in the EEA is Dorling Kindersley
Verlag GmbH. Arnulfstr. 124, 80636 Munich, Germany

A catalog record for this book
is available from the Library of Congress.
ISBN 978-0-7440-8836-6

DK books are available at special discounts when purchased
in bulk for sales promotions, premiums, fund-raising, or educational
use. For details, contact SpecialSales@dk.com

Printed and bound in China

Photo credits:
Cover photo © 2023 by Will "SimplisticPhobia" Jenkins
Pages 2, 3, 5, 14, 16, 17, 18, 57, 88, 114, 142, 169, 189, 205, 220, 255
© 2023 by Will "SimplisticPhobia" Jenkins
All other images © 2023 by Jonathan Cooper

For the curious
www.dk.com

To my loved ones who are still here with us and those who have passed—this is for the family!

CONTENTS

SIDES

SWEET TREATS

SIGNATURE DRINKS

SAUCES

INTRODUCTION

SO, WHERE DO WE BEGIN?

First and foremost, I would like to thank each and every person reading this right now, because that means you took the time to share a moment with me and enjoy all that this book has to offer! If you love to cook, enjoy sharing a meal with family and friends, or simply just like to *eat*, you're in the right place.

There is nothing better than a good meal, and a good meal is something you will never forget. Sometimes the good meals are the expensive ones, and sometimes they're the most affordable, simplest meals you've ever had. But even if you have a ton of different ingredients, cheap or expensive, the ingredients by themselves usually won't amount to much. When you mix them together, throw them into a pot, and cook them up, you can create a masterpiece. If I just have flour, I can't do much, but give me a couple of eggs, a few splashes of milk, a little sugar—now we're making a cake.

That's where my slogan, *somethin' outta nothin'*, comes from. When my brothers and I were growing up, my father would always say this to us. When we couldn't find anything we wanted to eat in the kitchen, he would always tell us, "There's something in there you can eat; you just gotta look." That stuck with me forever, Pops!

So we would look, find the most random ingredients, and make the most delicious meal—every time! Whether it was something simple, like a fried bologna sandwich with a side of whatever you could find, or something more complex, like a stir fry with a bunch of different ingredients, it was always delicious. All I'm going to say is a little creativity can take you a looooong way. Cooking has always played a huge part in my family's life, whether we were cooking a traditional holiday meal or just figuring out what to eat at a random weekend cookout. Food always brought us together.

Growing up, I always loved to cook or just be around food in general—it was so interesting to me, and the possibilities were endless. One of my earliest memories of cooking is with my grandmother. I was barely tall enough to reach the counter, but I fondly remember making homemade meatballs with her. This was my first time cooking in the kitchen with her, but I was always asking her to make me something to eat as early as I can remember. When I was about six years old, I started telling everyone I wanted to be a chef when I grew up—look how things came full circle! Along the way, I went from wanting to be a banker, then wanting to be a physical therapist, and finally back to cooking.

It all started back in college. When my daughter was born and I was a young father, I immediately began thinking of ways to support her. I knew I could cook, and I wanted to see if I could make something happen with my natural talent! I called up about ten friends, made to-go plates for them, and charged them each five dollars. It was enough to cover the cost of the food, and all I needed was for each of them to spread the word. From there, things spread like wildfire!

I started a food delivery and catering business, driving around in my old '98 Toyota and selling food to college kids. Sometimes I would only sell enough to break even on the money I had spent on the food. Every now and then, it would be profitable, but it was always a gamble. I kept going, eventually

transforming my food delivery business into a private dinner business. At this point in my journey, I not only learned more than ever, but I also really started having fun with it. Imagine being able to do what you love, support your family, and keep taking things further and further—it sounds lovely, doesn't it?

Now this isn't to say stepping into doing private dinners was a complete cake walk. I had to learn to crawl, then walk, then run. But one of the most enjoyable parts of doing private dinners was just connecting and relating with people. I am such a people person, and being able to create a great meal, create a memory, and get to know the people I was cooking for was so rewarding! Perfecting my craft, experimenting, and soaking up game from all different walks of life by conducting private

dinners was pivotal in getting me where I am today: Eatwitzo.

When I graduated from college, I was able to take my career in the food industry by full storm. I had always felt like I had a restraint on me, having to do private dinners on the weekends, and then making sure I had my assignments turned in by 11:59 p.m. and going to class at 8 a.m. But I started posting on social media, @eatwitzo, and after a year of consistency, I finally had my breakthrough. My first viral moment happened so quickly—I was just recipe testing something one night and recorded it—and the rest was history. I went from a couple thousand supporters, to a hundred thousand, to a million, all in a matter of months!

I was able to keep falling in love with creating new and exciting food recipes, sharing them with the world, and making cooking fun. Learning how to make recipes completely from scratch is definitely one of the more satisfying parts about what I do. I'm the first to admit that I don't know how to cook everything to perfection. (White rice is my kryptonite!) But there is nothing more rewarding than recreating a specific dish that is close to someone's heart, making a video about it, and absolutely knocking it out of the park!

It's important to show people that some of their favorites can be made as easy as one, two, three—and that is one of the things that truly keeps me going. To this day, I still have to pinch myself because life happened so fast, but at the same time, I vividly remember how much I had to push myself day in and day out to become the person I am today. The moral of the story is KEEP GOING! I am completely self-taught when it comes to cooking, so there was

a lot of trial and error involved. I wouldn't be here today without a huge amount of help from my grandmothers and mother, of course—without them, there is no Eatwitzo! That's where my inspiration to cook comes from primarily: the Queens of the family.

As you make your way through this book, take a moment, enjoy it, and feel like you're right here with me cooking some amazing meals! Good food brings people together and creates memories to last a lifetime. This book is a piece of me, written for you and your stomachs to enjoy! Thank you all once again for sharing this moment with me. From my kitchen to yours, I present *Somethin' Outta Nothin'*. Enjoy!

—Eatwitzo (Zo)

KITCHEN ESSENTIALS

Here are the items you'll need to make miracles in the kitchen:

GOOD KNIVES

Sharp knives will make your cooking process one thousand percent easier. My go-tos are a classic chef's knife and a small paring knife. Sometimes you need something smaller to get the job done.

RUBBER SPATULAS

Trust me. It helps in ways you wouldn't imagine. Rubber spatulas help you scrape the sides of a bowl or pan, making sure you don't miss a drop. Nothing goes to waste!

CAST-IRON SKILLETS & SAUTÉ PANS

A good, seasoned cast-iron skillet is essential, and if it's been passed down to you, even better. A good sauté pan will get the job done, and for certain recipes, the end result is better if you cook the entire recipe in the same pan to retain all of the flavor. Here are a few more specific pans for you to add to your essentials:

- Cast-iron skillets: 8-inch, 9-inch, and 10-inch
- Sauté pans: 10-inch, 11-inch, and 12-inch
- Large pot or Dutch oven
- Small and medium saucepans

CUTTING BOARDS

This one is important—there's nothing like having a good cutting board when preparing food. Make sure you have at least two or three: one for meats, one for vegetables, and one for everything else.

BAKING PANS

A strong variety will enhance your cooking experience! There's nothing worse than trying to create a meal and not having the right pans—or not having enough pans. Here are some of the essentials for the recipes in this book:

- Bundt cake or pound cake pan
- Springform pan (for cheesecakes)
- 9-inch square baking dish
- Rimmed baking sheets
- Wire cooling racks
- Muffin pans
- Outdoor grill (this one isn't required, but it's recommended) or grill pan

OVEN MITTS

So you don't burn yourself!

SEASONINGS & SAUCES

Can't make the recipes without them! Garlic powder, onion powder, salt, and black pepper are the essential staples for this book. This is what I like to call the seasoning starter kit. Other seasoning staples include:

SEASONINGS

- Bay leaves
- Cajun seasoning
- Cayenne
- Chili powder
- Cumin
- Dried dill
- Italian seasoning
- Old Bay seasoning
- Dried oregano
- Paprika
- Red pepper flakes
- Sazón
- Smoked paprika

SAUCES

- Honey
- Hot sauce
- Ketchup
- Mayonnaise
- Mustard
- Worcestershire sauce

OILS

- Olive oil
- Neutral frying oil (of your preference—I like canola oil)
- Baking spray

BAKING

You can't make my sweet treats without these staples!

- All-purpose flour
- Baking powder
- Baking soda
- Cornstarch

EXTRACTS

- Almond
- Vanilla

SPICES

- Ground cinnamon
- Ground ginger
- Ground nutmeg

SUGARS

- Brown
- Granulated
- Powdered

FRIDGE

Grab these items from the refrigerated section!

- Butter
- Buttermilk
- Eggs
- Heavy cream
- Milk
- Sour cream

CHEESES

- Cheddar
- Cream cheese
- Colby Jack
- Parmesan
- Pepper Jack

CLEANUP

No matter how good you are at cooking, cleaning is always at the other end of a good meal. Here's what you need to make the process as easy as possible:

- Broom and dustpan
- Dish soap
- Kitchen towels
- Paper towels
- Sponges
- Surface cleaner (also helps with cross-contamination when cooking)
- Scented candle (can't light it until everything is squeaky clean!)

MUSIC

There's nothing like vibing to some tunes while throwing down in the kitchen, whether it's R&B, hip hop, country, pop, or jazz. Sometimes a good song just gets you in the zone and adds a little bit of razzle dazzle to the meal!

Personally, I enjoy some nice R&B, a good drink, and something fun to cook. The best part is finishing with a clean kitchen, a lit candle, and a delicious plate in front of me.

MENUS FOR EVERY OCCASION

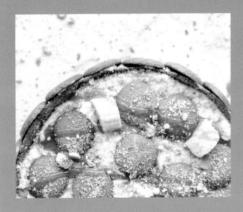

DATE NIGHTS

No need to go out and spend money on fancy dinners—make a reservation at home! This is my ideal selection for a perfect night in. Thank me later—date night will never be boring again.

- ◆ **Appetizer:** Crab Cake Stuffed Cheddar Biscuits (page 89)

- ◆ **Entree:** Lamb Chop & Salmon Surf 'n' Turf Pasta (page 127)

- ◆ **Side:** Apple-Bacon Brussels Sprouts (page 171)

- ◆ **Dessert:** No-Bake Banana Pudding Cheesecake (page 208)

- ◆ **Cocktail:** Eatwitzo Special (page 233)

FAMILY STYLE

When it's time to sit at the table as a family, you have to have a good meal! In my household growing up, it was always a good Sunday dinner. Here are a few of my favorite dishes to create that family dinner magic:

- ◆ **Five-Cheese Mac & Cheese** (page 168)

- ◆ **Smothered Pork Chops** (page 148) over white rice

- ◆ **Honey Jalapeño Cornbread** (page 175)

- ◆ **Southern-Style Fried Cabbage with Sausage, Bacon & Peppers** (page 172)

- ◆ **Arroz con Gandules** (page 183)

There are so many recipes to help gather the family around the table and enjoy an amazing meal.

PARTIES

Whether you're hosting or in charge of bringing something to contribute, a party has to have good food! Since I'm usually the host, here are some of my favorite party dishes!

- ◆ **Cajun Crab & Shrimp Spinach Dip** (page 65): Gotta have a dip. Dips are the life of the party, easy to make, filling, and usually one of the most memorable dishes!

- ◆ **Honey Fried Chicken Wings** (page 120): What's a party without wings? You can never have enough. So when you think you have enough, double the recipe!

- ◆ **Cheesy Shrimp Empanadas** (page 86): At any family event of mine, the empanadas *have* to be there! My mom is usually in the kitchen making dozens of them, but we all pitch in so we can enjoy the end result.

- ◆ **Strawberry Cream Cheese Donut Holes** (page 199): Need a dessert to feed a crowd? Look no further—these are the perfect bite-size desserts!

- ◆ **Holiday Party Punch** (page 222): This one is for when you have to pull out the big pitchers for the holidays. Make a big batch, give everyone a cup, and enjoy spending time with family and friends.

- ◆ **Watermelon Lemon Drops** (page 229): I can smell the grill and hear the music playing already! These are the perfect addition to any party; they are refreshing and delicious.

BREAKFAST

For me, breakfast has always been one of the most important meals of the day. It sounds cliché, I know, but honestly, is there a better way to wake up then to the smell of bacon, fluffy waffles, or something fresh out of the oven? You'll be floating into the kitchen still half asleep!

My favorite memories of eating breakfast as a kid are from summers with my grandmother. My brothers and I spent countless summers down in Kissimmee, Florida, with my grandmother and grandfather (we call them Ma and Pop Pop). While my grandfather would get up and head to work, my grandmother would wake us up to the smell of three very specific foods: blueberry muffins, sausage patties, and eggs.

To some, this may seem very simple, but when I tell you nothing is better than waking up to a fresh breakfast every morning, nothing is better! We definitely were early birds (well, most of us— my older brother always liked to sleep all day!), so the best part was that you could wake up, eat a small plate, relax, and go back for seconds all before 10 a.m.!

A good breakfast, no matter how early or late you enjoy it, is always going to be the perfect start to any day. And I can't end this without giving my late great-grandmother her time to shine as well. Every. Single. Morning. She would cook a full breakfast for anyone that was in her house! She cooked everything: bacon or sausage, homemade southern biscuits, savory grits, and, of course, eggs. No matter what, you would be fed and ready to start your day. The recipes in this chapter are inspired by these breakfast memories. So, enjoy them, take a moment to relax, and start the day off right!

BANANAS FOSTER FRENCH TOAST

4 TO 5 SERVINGS	PREP: 10 MINUTES	COOK: 30 MINUTES

INGREDIENTS

Banana Topping
1 tablespoon butter

½ cup brown sugar

¼ cup dark rum

1 to 2 bananas, peeled and sliced

½ cup pecans

1 teaspoon ground cinnamon

1 teaspoon vanilla extract

French Toast
3 large eggs

1 cup heavy cream

2 teaspoons ground cinnamon

2 teaspoons vanilla extract

½ teaspoon ground nutmeg

Butter

1 loaf brioche-style bread,
  thickly sliced

If you can't decide between waffles and pancakes, French toast is the perfect middleman! It's actually one of the foods that I'm not the best at cooking, but don't worry, I perfected this recipe! I've found that stale bread works best, and make sure the slices don't get too soggy in the custard. Fresh fruit was made to pair with this French toast.

1   **Make the banana topping:** To a small saucepan over medium-low heat, add the butter and brown sugar. Cook until the sugar has dissolved and a syrup begins to form, 2 to 3 minutes.

2   Bring the pan to a low simmer and add the rum. Cook until the alcohol has evaporated, about 3 minutes. Add the bananas, pecans, cinnamon, and vanilla. Mix well, being careful not to break up the bananas, then remove the pan from the heat.

3   **Make the French toast:** In a small bowl, combine the eggs, cream, cinnamon, vanilla, and nutmeg to make a custard.

4   Set a large pan over medium heat and add about 2 teaspoons of butter. Dip the brioche slices into the custard, then add to the pan. Cook until a golden-brown crust has formed, 2 to 3 minutes per side. Remove from the pan. Repeat with more butter and the remaining bread slices.

5   Pour the banana mixture over the toast and enjoy!

CLASSIC FRIED CHICKEN WINGS & WAFFLES

3 TO 4 SERVINGS	PREP: 30 MINUTES	COOK: 40 MINUTES

INGREDIENTS

Chicken Wings

Neutral oil, for frying

2 cups all-purpose flour

1 tablespoon cayenne

1 tablespoon garlic powder

1 tablespoon Italian seasoning

1 tablespoon onion powder

1 tablespoon paprika

1 tablespoon black pepper

1½ teaspoons salt (optional)

6 whole chicken wings

¼ cup yellow mustard

1½ teaspoons sazón

Waffles

2 cups all-purpose flour

2 tablespoons sugar

2 teaspoons baking powder

1 teaspoon ground cinnamon

½ teaspoon salt

1½ cups milk

2 large eggs

10 tablespoons unsalted butter, melted

1 teaspoon vanilla extract

¼ teaspoon almond extract (optional)

Maple syrup

Powdered sugar

Perfect for breakfast or dinner, this recipe is a certified classic. There's no better way to describe chicken and waffles: They are deliciously salty, sweet, and savory at the same time. Drizzle a little syrup on the chicken, and make sure you get syrup, chicken, and waffle in every bite. Who knew combining these two foods would create this masterpiece of a dish?

1 **Make the chicken wings:** Fill a large pot halfway with oil and heat to 375°F.

2 In a large bowl, combine the flour, cayenne, garlic powder, Italian seasoning, onion powder, paprika, black pepper, and salt, if using.

3 In another large bowl, combine the chicken wings, mustard, and sazón. Coat the chicken evenly and generously, to help the flour stick.

4 Toss the chicken in the flour mixture, ensuring every piece is covered. Drop the chicken into the oil and fry until extra crispy and floating, 5 to 7 minutes.

5 Meanwhile, preheat your waffle iron.

6 **Make the waffles:** In a medium bowl, combine the flour, sugar, baking powder, cinnamon, and salt. In a large bowl, combine the milk, eggs, butter, vanilla, and almond extract, if using.

7 Add the dry ingredients to the wet ingredients and mix well.

8 Pour the batter into the waffle iron and cook until the waffles are crispy and golden brown, about 3 minutes, depending on your waffle maker.

9 Place the chicken wings on top of the waffles and drizzle with maple syrup. Top with powdered sugar, and enjoy!

LEMON BLUEBERRY PANCAKES

3 TO 4 SERVINGS	PREP: 25 MINUTES	COOK: 30 MINUTES

INGREDIENTS

Blueberry Glaze

1½ cups blueberries

¼ cup sugar

1 tablespoon cornstarch

Sprinkle of lemon zest

Juice of ½ lemon

½ teaspoon vanilla extract

Pancakes

1½ cups all-purpose flour

1 tablespoon lemon zest

1 tablespoon sugar

2 teaspoons baking powder

¼ teaspoon salt

Butter

1¼ cups milk

1 large egg

Juice of ½ lemon

½ teaspoon vanilla extract

Two of the best fruits combine with some delicious pancakes! Blueberries are one of my favorite fruits to pair with desserts. (I love strawberries, too, but sometimes they get a little boring!) A major key to making the best pancakes is to ensure the pan is hot enough to give you delicious crispy edges as well as a fluffy, golden-brown center. Use fresh butter to cook each pancake: It makes all the difference.

1   **Make the blueberry glaze:** To a small saucepan over medium heat, add the blueberries, ½ cup water, and sugar. Cook until the blueberries begin to break down and the sugar and water have combined, 3 to 5 minutes.

2   Mix the cornstarch and 1 tablespoon of water in a small bowl to create a slurry.

3   Reduce the heat to low and add the slurry, lemon zest, lemon juice, and vanilla. Cook until thickened, 2 to 3 minutes, then remove from the heat.

4   **Make the pancakes:** In a large bowl, combine the flour, lemon zest, sugar, baking powder, and salt.

5   Melt 2 tablespoons of butter, then add to another large bowl. Add the milk, egg, lemon juice, and vanilla extract to the butter and mix.

6   Add the dry ingredients to the wet ingredients and combine. It will be lumpy, so don't overmix.

7   To a large pan over medium heat, add just enough butter to coat the bottom of the pan, then add about ¼ cup batter for each pancake. Cook until bubbles form on the top of the pancakes, 2 to 3 minutes, then flip and cook until golden brown, 2 to 3 more minutes. Remove from the pan.

8   Repeat step 7 with more butter and the remaining pancake batter.

9   Serve immediately, topped with the blueberry glaze. Enjoy!

BREAKFAST EGG BOMBS

6 TO 8 SERVINGS	PREP: 15 MINUTES	COOK: 30 MINUTES

INGREDIENTS

1 pound pork or turkey
   country sausage

12 large eggs

1 cup shredded cheddar

1 cup baby spinach, chopped

1 medium tomato, diced

½ cup heavy cream

1 teaspoon black pepper

1 teaspoon garlic powder

1 teaspoon onion powder

½ teaspoon red pepper flakes

½ teaspoon salt

This is my favorite grab-and-go breakfast. It's fully customizable, easy to make, and easy to clean up! Imagine an omelet loaded with all of your favorite ingredients and packed into a small handheld meal. Refrigerate or freeze, then pop them in the microwave or air fryer for a couple minutes and head out the door!

1   Preheat the oven to 375°F. Line two 12-cup muffin pans with liners.

2   Heat a medium skillet over medium heat. Add the sausage and cook until browned and cooked through, breaking up the meat as it cooks, 6 to 8 minutes. Drain the excess grease.

3   In a large bowl, whisk the eggs. Add the sausage, cheddar, spinach, tomato, heavy cream, black pepper, garlic powder, onion powder, red pepper flakes, and salt. Whisk to combine.

4   Fill the cupcake liners about three-fourths of the way with the mixture. Bake for 15 to 20 minutes, until golden brown on top.

5   Allow to cool for up to 30 minutes before serving. Enjoy!

Pro Tip

Freeze these egg bombs in a freezer-safe bag and warm up in the microwave or air fryer for a few minutes for a bite on the go!

CRUMBLE COFFEE CAKE

| 9 SERVINGS | PREP: 25 MINUTES | COOK: 30 MINUTES |

INGREDIENTS

Baking spray or shortening

All-purpose flour, for dusting

Crumble Topping

¾ cup all-purpose flour

⅔ cup packed dark brown sugar

6 tablespoons cold unsalted butter, diced (see Pro Tip 1)

1½ teaspoons ground cinnamon

¼ teaspoon ground nutmeg

Coffee Cake

1⅓ cups all-purpose flour

1 teaspoon baking powder

¼ teaspoon baking soda

¼ teaspoon salt

¾ cup sugar

8 tablespoons unsalted butter, softened

2 tablespoons whole or 2 percent milk

1 teaspoon vanilla extract

½ teaspoon almond extract

2 large eggs, at room temperature

⅓ cup sour cream

Honey (optional)

When I was a kid, this was easily my favorite "breakfast"—if you can even call it that, because this recipe deserves a spot on the dessert table at every family get-together. The funny thing about this cake is that nobody ever made it at home, so I would always order it at restaurants or pick it up at convenience stores. Enjoy this with a hot cup of coffee or wash it down with a cold iced coffee—whatever you prefer!

1 Preheat the oven to 350°F. Grease an 8-inch square baking pan lightly with baking spray and dust lightly with flour.

2 **Make the crumble:** In a small bowl, combine the flour, brown sugar, butter, cinnamon, and nutmeg. Use a pastry cutter or a fork to mix the ingredients to form a crumbly texture (see Pro Tip 1).

3 **Make the cake:** In a medium bowl, mix the flour, baking powder, baking soda, and salt.

4 In a large bowl, mix the sugar, butter, milk vanilla, and almond extract (see Pro Tip 2). Add the eggs and sour cream and mix until fully incorporated.

5 Slowly add in the dry ingredients, mixing until everything is just incorporated. The batter should not be smooth; be careful not to overmix.

6 Spread half of the batter into the pan, followed by half of the crumble topping, then repeat, ending with the crumble on top.

7 Bake for 30 to 40 minutes, until a toothpick inserted into the center comes out clean. Let cool completely before slicing.

8 Drizzle lightly with honey, if desired, and enjoy!

Pro Tips

1. Cold butter is necessary to help the crumble topping hold together.

2. Feel free to use a stand or hand mixer for this step!

DEEP-FRIED GRIT CAKES
WITH CREAMY SHRIMP SAUCE

6 SERVINGS	PREP: 5 MINUTES, PLUS 1 HOUR COOLING TIME	COOK: 1 HOUR

INGREDIENTS

Grits

1 quart chicken broth

1 cup quick 5-minute grits

¼ cup shredded Colby Jack

¼ cup heavy cream

2 tablespoons butter

1 teaspoon black pepper

¼ teaspoon salt

Neutral oil, for frying

1 cup all-purpose flour

2 eggs, whisked

1 cup breadcrumbs

Shrimp Sauce

1 pound large shrimp, peeled and deveined

1½ teaspoons garlic powder, divided

1½ teaspoons onion powder, divided

1½ teaspoons paprika, divided

1½ teaspoons black pepper, divided

5 strips bacon, diced

¾ cup heavy cream

½ cup diced bell pepper, any color

1 tablespoon tomato paste

½ teaspoon cayenne

½ teaspoon salt

Chopped fresh parsley

Everyone knows and loves classic shrimp and grits, or even fried fish and grits, right? Now imagine taking the creamy grits, deep-frying them to get a nice crust, and then pouring a savory shrimp sauce right on top of the golden brown grits. It sounds amazing, right? Go ahead and try this recipe—you can thank me later!

1 **Make the grits:** Bring the chicken broth to a boil in a medium pot. Whisk in the grits, then reduce the heat to a low simmer. Stir occasionally until the broth is fully absorbed and the grits have thickened, 5 to 7 minutes.

2 Add the Colby Jack, heavy cream, butter, black pepper, and salt. Transfer the grits to a 9-inch square baking dish and place them in the fridge to cool completely and firm up, at least 1 hour.

3 Fill a medium pot halfway with oil and heat to 375°F.

4 Cut the grit cakes into 3-inch squares. Fill a shallow bowl with the flour, another with the eggs, and a third with the breadcrumbs. Coat the cakes in the flour, then in the eggs, and then in the breadcrumbs. Fry until golden brown and crispy, 2 to 3 minutes.

5 **Make the shrimp sauce:** Season the shrimp with 1 teaspoon each of garlic powder, onion powder, paprika, and black pepper.

6 To a large pan over medium heat, add the bacon and cook until crispy, about 5 minutes. Remove the bacon from the pan and drain most of the grease. Reserve about ¼ cup bacon for serving.

7 Add the shrimp and cook until pink, 1 to 2 minutes on each side. Remove the shrimp from the pan and add the bell pepper. Cook until tender, 1 to 2 minutes.

8 Stir in the tomato paste, then add the heavy cream and the remaining ½ teaspoon each of garlic powder, onion powder, paprika, and black pepper, along with the cayenne and salt.

9 Simmer over low heat until the sauce begins to bubble and thicken, 3 to 4 minutes. Add the bacon and shrimp back to the pan.

10 Top the grit cakes with the creamy shrimp sauce and garnish with parsley and reserved bacon. Enjoy!

ULTIMATE BREAKFAST SKILLET

3 TO 4 SERVINGS	PREP: 20 MINUTES	COOK: 45 MINUTES

INGREDIENTS

4 strips thick-cut bacon

½ pound ground pork breakfast sausage

2 tablespoons butter

3 medium russet potatoes, diced

1 small bell pepper, diced

½ small onion, diced

1½ teaspoons garlic powder

1 teaspoon onion powder

1 teaspoon black pepper

1 teaspoon smoked paprika

½ teaspoon salt

3 jumbo eggs

¾ cup shredded Colby Jack

Chopped fresh parsley

This is my kind of breakfast. While sweet breakfast dishes are great, I am definitely a savory type of person. Pass me the bacon, eggs, hash browns, sausage, and a piece of toast or a biscuit. Anybody with me? The beautiful thing about this skillet is that you can add pretty much whatever leftovers you have in your refrigerator into a pan, season it up, crack a few eggs, and breakfast is served!

1   To a large pan over medium heat, add the bacon and cook until crispy, about 7 minutes. Transfer to a plate, then add the sausage to the pan and cook until browned and well done, 6 to 8 minutes. Transfer to the plate with the bacon.

2   Wipe the grease from the pan, then add the butter and the potatoes. Cook until the edges begin to get crispy, 5 minutes, then add the bell pepper and onion.

3   Cook until the potatoes are fork-tender and the pepper and onion are soft, about 6 minutes. (Covering the pan briefly with a lid can help to ensure a perfectly tender potato!)

4   Add the garlic powder, onion powder, black pepper, paprika, and salt. Toss thoroughly, then add the sausage and bacon, breaking the bacon into large crumbles.

5   Create three pockets in the mixture, then crack the eggs into them. Sprinkle on the cheese and cover the pan. Allow the eggs to cook and the cheese to melt for 3 minutes for a runnier egg yolk and up to 5 minutes for a firmer egg yolk.

6   Garnish with fresh parsley and enjoy!

APPLE CINNAMON MUFFINS

18 MUFFINS	PREP: 35 MINUTES	COOK: 30 MINUTES

INGREDIENTS

Muffins

Baking spray or cupcake liners

2 cups all-purpose flour

2 teaspoons ground cinnamon

1 teaspoon baking powder

½ teaspoon ground nutmeg

¼ teaspoon salt

2 small Granny Smith apples, diced (about 2 cups)

8 tablespoons butter, melted

1 cup granulated sugar

2 large eggs

½ cup milk

1½ teaspoons vanilla extract

½ teaspoon almond extract

Crumble Topping

1½ cups all-purpose flour

¼ cup brown sugar

¼ cup granulated sugar

1 egg

1 teaspoon vanilla extract

½ teaspoon baking powder

½ teaspoon salt

8 tablespoons cold butter, diced

Whoever decided to mix apple and cinnamon together knew what they were doing! Muffins are a great grab-and-go breakfast, because they're easy to transport, filling, and delicious! Pair one of these muffins with your favorite fruit and you have a breakfast of champions. (P.S. They also make a great late-night snack!)

1 Preheat the oven to 350°F. Spray one 12-cup and one 6-cup muffin pan with baking spray or line with liners.

2 **Make the muffins:** In a large bowl, combine the flour, cinnamon, baking powder, nutmeg, and salt. Stir in the apples.

3 In another large bowl, combine the butter, sugar, eggs, milk, vanilla, and almond extract. Slowly incorporate the dry ingredients into the wet ingredients and mix until well incorporated.

4 **Make the crumble topping:** In a third bowl, combine the flour, brown sugar, granulated sugar, egg, vanilla, baking powder, and salt. Add the butter and mix thoroughly by pressing the ingredients together with your fingers to form a crumble (see Pro Tip).

5 Fill the muffin cups three-fourths of the way with the batter, then add the crumble on top.

6 Bake for 30 minutes, until the tops are browned and a toothpick comes out clean. Enjoy!

Pro Tip

If the mixture is too doughy, slowly add in tablespoons of flour until a soft crumble begins to form.

BREAKFAST CHORIZO TACOS

10 TACOS	PREP: 10 MINUTES	COOK: 20 MINUTES

INGREDIENTS

Creamy Salsa
1 cup tomato salsa
½ cup sour cream
1 tablespoon lime juice
1 teaspoon chili powder

10 white corn or flour street tortillas
1 pound ground chorizo
4 eggs, whisked
½ cup shredded Colby Jack
1 avocado, thinly sliced

Tacos for breakfast? Yes, please! These tacos are filling and simply delicious. Think of these tacos as smaller, scaled down versions of a traditional breakfast burrito. Add on some crispy bacon bits if you're feeling fancy—all the different textures will blend perfectly together!

1 **Make the creamy salsa:** To a small bowl, add the salsa, sour cream, lime juice, and chili powder. Mix well. Add 2 tablespoons of water, 1 tablespoon at a time, until the consistency is smooth and thin.

2 To a medium pan over medium heat, add the chorizo and cook until slightly charred and cooked through, 5 to 7 minutes. Transfer to a plate.

3 In batches, add the tortillas to the pan and lightly toast them to soak up all of the flavor from the chorizo, about 30 seconds per side. Transfer to a plate.

4 Add the eggs to the pan and scramble, 2 to 3 minutes.

5 **Assemble the tacos:** Start with a tortilla, then add eggs, cheese, chorizo, avocado, and salsa. Repeat with the remaining ingredients. Enjoy!

OLD SCHOOL SAUSAGE GRAVY BREAKFAST PIZZA

2 PIZZAS	PREP: 15 MINUTES	COOK: 25 MINUTES

INGREDIENTS

1 pound ground pork breakfast sausage

2 tablespoons all-purpose flour

1½ cups half and half

1½ teaspoons black pepper

1½ teaspoons rubbed sage

1 teaspoon chili powder

¼ teaspoon red pepper flakes

5 strips thick-cut bacon

1 tablespoon butter

5 large eggs, whisked

2 large premade pizza crusts

1½ cups shredded Colby Jack or mozzarella

Chopped fresh parsley

I know I'm not the only one who used to eat the sausage and egg breakfast pizza in grade school! This delicious concoction of sausage gravy, scrambled eggs, and bacon on a pizza crust used to be the highlight of school mornings. Take a trip down memory lane with me!

1   Preheat the oven to 400°F.

2   In a large pan over medium heat, cook the sausage until browned and cooked through, breaking it into small pieces with a spatula, 5 to 7 minutes.

3   Sprinkle in the flour and stir to coat. Reduce the heat to medium-low, then slowly stir in the half and half until you get a smooth, gravy-like consistency.

4   Reduce the heat to low, then add the pepper, sage, chili powder, and red pepper flakes. Adjust the seasoning to taste, then set aside.

5   Cook the bacon in another medium pan over medium heat, flipping occasionally, until crispy, 5 to 7 minutes.

6   Remove the bacon from the pan, wipe out the grease, and add the butter. Once the butter has melted, add the eggs and scramble softly until fully cooked, 3 to 4 minutes.

7   Spread the sausage gravy evenly onto the pizza crusts. Add the eggs and evenly spread on the cheese. Crumble the bacon on top.

8   Bake the pizzas directly on the oven rack for about 5 minutes, until the cheese has melted. Garnish with fresh parsley and enjoy!

HOT HONEY DRIZZLE FRIED CHICKEN BISCUITS

3 SERVINGS	PREP: 40 MINUTES	COOK: 35 MINUTES

INGREDIENTS

Biscuits

2¼ cups all-purpose flour, plus more for dusting

1½ tablespoon baking powder

1 teaspoon salt

10 tablespoons cold butter, diced

1 cup cold buttermilk

Fried Chicken

Neutral oil, for frying

1 pound chicken breast

1 cup cold buttermilk

½ cup hot sauce

2 cups all-purpose flour

1 tablespoon cayenne

1 tablespoon garlic powder

1 tablespoon Italian seasoning

1 tablespoon onion powder

1 tablespoon paprika

1 tablespoon black pepper

1½ teaspoons sazón

1½ teaspoons salt

Hot Honey

1 cup honey

½ cup hot sauce

Hot Honey Fried Salmon Biscuits

These hot honey chicken biscuits are amazing, but what about hot honey fried salmon biscuits? For my seafood lovers out there, give this a try: Make the salmon from the Fried Salmon BLT (page 111) in place of the chicken and thank me later!

The only thing better than a sausage biscuit for breakfast is a chicken biscuit. And this hot honey drizzle takes it to a new level! Making homemade biscuits reminds me of my great-grandmother, who would make us fresh, Southern-style biscuits every morning to go with breakfast. Enjoy this recipe and take a second to live in the moment!

1 Preheat the oven to 425°F.

2 **Make the biscuits:** In a large bowl, mix the flour, baking powder, and salt.

3 Add the butter and use a pastry cutter or fork to cut the butter into the flour until the butter is well incorporated and small flakes begin to form. Fold in the buttermilk slowly to form a somewhat sticky dough.

4 Coat a surface with flour. Form the dough into a rectangle and roll it about 1 to 1½ inches thick. Use a biscuit cutter or drinking glass to cut the dough into 2- to 3-inch circles. Transfer to a baking sheet and bake for 10 to 15 minutes, until the tops are lightly brown.

5 **Make the chicken:** Fill a medium pot halfway with oil and heat to 375°F. Cut the chicken into 2- to 3-inch pieces (see Pro Tip).

6 In a large bowl, combine the chicken, buttermilk, and hot sauce.

7 In a separate container, combine the flour, cayenne, garlic powder, Italian seasoning, onion powder, paprika, black pepper, sazón, and salt. Mix well.

8 Dip the chicken into the flour mixture and turn to coat thoroughly. Set aside for a few minutes before frying.

9 Fry the chicken until it is crispy and begins to float to the top of the oil, 5 to 6 minutes.

10 **Make the hot honey:** Mix the honey and hot sauce in a small bowl. Microwave for 30 seconds until warm and pour over the chicken. Top a biscuit with chicken and eat while warm. Enjoy!

Pro Tip

Cut the chicken into pieces that are about the same size as your biscuits for the best results.

SALMON CROQUETTES

12 CROQUETTES | PREP: 25 MINUTES | COOK: 15 MINUTES

INGREDIENTS

14 to 16 ounces canned salmon, deboned (see Pro Tips)

1 large egg

¼ cup diced yellow onion

¼ cup diced green bell pepper

1 tablespoon mayonnaise

1 tablespoon Worcestershire sauce

¼ cup breadcrumbs

1½ teaspoons all-purpose flour

1 teaspoon garlic powder

1 teaspoon onion powder

1 teaspoon black pepper

1 teaspoon smoked paprika

Neutral oil, for frying

Lemon wedges (optional)

Chopped fresh parsley

Salmon cakes, salmon patties, salmon croquettes—whatever you call them, just know they are simply to die for. While these are traditionally made with canned salmon, fresh salmon can take the flavor up a few notches (see Pro Tip 1)! Pair with some creamy grits or a slice of toast and a few splashes of hot sauce.

1 Add the salmon to a large bowl and mash with a fork. Add the egg, onion, bell pepper, mayonnaise, and Worcestershire sauce. Mix well.

2 Add the breadcrumbs, flour, garlic powder, onion powder, black pepper, and paprika. Give everything a final mix and form into patties, each about ¼ cup in size. Place the patties in the fridge for a few minutes to firm up.

3 Fill a medium pan with about ½ inch of oil and heat to 375°F.

4 Fry the patties until crispy and brown, 2 to 3 minutes per side.

5 Remove from the oil, squeeze on a splash of lemon juice, if desired, and sprinkle on parsley. Enjoy!

Pro Tips

1 To substitute fresh salmon in this recipe, cook 16 ounces of skinless salmon to your preference and begin with step 1.

2 Feel free to leave the bones in if you wish; after cooking, they will be soft enough to eat.

SWEET POTATO STUFFED FRENCH TOAST

4 TO 5 SERVINGS	PREP: 25 MINUTES	COOK: 15 MINUTES

INGREDIENTS

Filling

1 cup cooked sweet potato

½ cup brown sugar

1 teaspoon ground cinnamon

1 teaspoon vanilla extract

½ teaspoon ground nutmeg

¼ teaspoon ground cloves

Custard

1 cup heavy cream

4 large eggs

1 teaspoon ground cinnamon

1 teaspoon vanilla extract

1 teaspoon hazelnut syrup

5 thick slices brioche-style bread

5 teaspoons unsalted butter

Salted caramel or maple syrup

Powdered sugar

This recipe almost landed in the dessert section! Imagine all the flavors of a sweet potato pie, but for breakfast. If that doesn't intrigue you, I don't know what will! Don't feel guilty eating this for breakfast—I promise it's not dessert!

1   **Make the filling:** In a small bowl, combine the sweet potato, brown sugar, cinnamon, vanilla, nutmeg, and cloves. Mix well. Transfer the mixture into a small sandwich bag and cut a small opening in one of the bottom corners.

2   **Make the custard:** In a wide, shallow bowl, combine the heavy cream, eggs, cinnamon, vanilla, and hazelnut syrup. Mix well.

3   Cut a small slit into the top of each slice of bread big enough to fit your sandwich bag tip.

4   Insert the tip of the sandwich bag into the opening in the bread, then add the sweet potato mixture, just until it starts to come out of the opening in the bread. Repeat with the remaining slices.

5   Heat 2 teaspoons butter in a large skillet over medium heat.

6   Lightly dip both sides of a stuffed bread slice into the custard (be careful not to soak too much or your French toast will get soggy), then place into the skillet. Repeat with another slice.

7   Cook until a nice golden-brown crust begins to form, about 3 minutes on each side. Transfer to a plate.

8   Repeat steps 5 to 7 with the remaining butter and bread slices. Garnish the French toast with extra sweet potato mixture as desired.

9   Top with salted caramel or syrup, sprinkle with powdered sugar, and dive in!

CRACKED CRAB LEGS & GRITS

4 TO 5 SERVINGS	PREP: 25 MINUTES	COOK: 35 MINUTES

INGREDIENTS

2 pounds snow crab legs

1 cup quick 5-minute grits

16 tablespoons unsalted butter, divided

½ cup shredded cheddar

1½ teaspoons garlic powder

1 teaspoon onion powder

1 teaspoon salt

½ teaspoon black pepper

½ teaspoon chili powder

2 tablespoons chopped fresh parsley

Hear me out: Seafood and grits are good no matter how you prepare them. So why not try crab and grits? This recipe takes a little more work than others, since you have to shell all of the crab legs. But I'm telling you, each bite will have you questioning where this dish has been all of your life!

1 Place a steamer insert in a large pot, then fill with water to the bottom of the steamer and bring to a boil. Add the crab legs and steam, in batches if needed, until the crab legs are fully heated, 5 to 10 minutes.

2 Carefully remove the crab meat from the legs with a crab cracker or your hands. Be sure to keep as much meat intact as possible (see Pro Tip). Discard the shells.

3 In a medium pot, bring 4 cups of water to a boil. Add the grits and continuously whisk until smooth. Reduce the heat to low and simmer until the grits are fully cooked, 5 to 10 minutes, whisking periodically. Keep over low heat until you are ready to eat.

4 Whisk in 8 tablespoons of butter, the cheddar, garlic powder, onion powder, salt, pepper, and chili powder to form a creamy, smooth consistency.

5 Place the grits into a large bowl. Place the cracked crab meat in a layer on top of the grits.

6 Microwave the remaining 8 tablespoons butter for 30 seconds or until melted. Gently pour the warm butter over the top of the crab meat to ensure every piece is covered. Sprinkle with parsley and enjoy while warm!

Pro Tip

The crab legs should pull easily from the shell; if they are stuck that means they were cooked too long.

SHAREABLES

Are they appetizers or shareables?

I guess it depends on how hungry you are!
Everyone has their preference on what appetizer
reigns supreme, so let's not get into that debate.
However, I think we all can agree that appetizers
are definitely the key component to any party or
get-together. They keep your belly full in
between cocktails or while you're watching your
favorite sports team dominate (if it's a losing
season, hang in there!). Variety is key!

The best part about appetizers is that you can
turn almost any food into one. You can repurpose
leftovers into something new, wrap whatever
filling you like into an egg roll, mix it together with
some cheese—the possibilities are endless!

Wings are probably the more versatile
appetizer—there's nearly an infinite amount of
flavor combinations. Let me see...you have lemon
pepper, garlic Parmesan, Buffalo, hot honey, BBQ,
teriyaki, mild, mango habanero... Let me stop
before I keep naming flavors for the rest of the
book! But one last question: Are you team drums
or flats?

TERIYAKI CHICKEN SKEWERS

7 SKEWERS	PREP: 30 MINUTES	COOK: 35 MINUTES

INGREDIENTS

1 pound chicken breast, cubed

¼ cup pineapple juice

1½ tablespoons diced chipotle peppers in adobo sauce

1½ teaspoons garlic powder

1½ teaspoons onion powder

1½ teaspoons white pepper

Chopped fresh parsley

Teriyaki Glaze

½ cup brown sugar

½ cup mirin

½ cup soy sauce

1 tablespoon ginger paste

1½ teaspoons garlic paste

1 tablespoon cornstarch

Wooden or metal skewers

Anything grilled on a skewer is an automatic *win* in my book. This recipe is great for grilling season, and if you want to jazz it up a bit, throw on some of your favorite vegetables! You can also use shrimp or steak as the protein for an amazing alternative.

1   In a large bowl, combine the chicken, pineapple juice, chipotle peppers, garlic powder, onion powder, and white pepper. Marinate for at least 15 minutes.

2   **Make the glaze:** In a medium saucepan over medium heat, combine the sugar, mirin, soy sauce, ½ cup water, ginger paste, and garlic paste. Mix thoroughly, then bring to a simmer.

3   Combine the cornstarch and 1 tablespoon of water in a small bowl to make a slurry. Add to the pan and allow the sauce to thicken for another 2 to 3 minutes. Remove from the heat.

4   Heat a grill or griddle pan to medium-high heat. Place the chicken onto skewers.

5   Add the skewers to the grill and cook until nicely seared on the bottom, 2 minutes.

6   Flip the skewers and baste with the glaze. Cook until charred, 2 to 3 minutes.

7   Flip once more and baste the other side, allowing the glaze to caramelize. Cook for 2 to 3 minutes, then remove from the heat and top with parsley.

CAJUN CRAB & SHRIMP SPINACH DIP

6 TO 8 SERVINGS	PREP: 25 MINUTES	COOK: 30 MINUTES

INGREDIENTS

2 tablespoons olive oil

1 pound small shrimp,
   peeled and deveined

One 13-ounce can water-packed
   quartered artichoke hearts, drained

12 ounces frozen chopped spinach,
   thawed

12 ounces cream cheese, softened

8 ounces lump crab meat, divided

1 tablespoon minced garlic

1 tablespoon garlic powder

1 tablespoon chili powder

1½ teaspoons Old Bay seasoning

1 teaspoon black pepper

1 teaspoon Cajun seasoning

1 teaspoon cayenne (optional)

1 teaspoon onion powder

1 teaspoon sazón

½ teaspoon paprika,
   plus more for serving

8 ounces shredded mozzarella

Chopped fresh parsley

Tortilla chips, for serving

Spinach dip is the king of appetizers and, quite frankly, it's not up for debate! It has the perfect amount of cheese and a bunch of vegetables, so that makes it healthy, right? Add the seafood and this appetizer will have you and your guests scraping the bowl for more!

1   Preheat the oven to 375°F.

2   Heat the olive oil in a small pan over medium heat. Add the shrimp and cook until pink on both sides, 2 to 3 minutes (see Pro Tip 1).

3   Thoroughly chop the artichoke hearts and add to a large bowl with the spinach. Use your hands to squeeze as much water out of the mixture as you can (you don't want your dip to be watery).

4   Add the cream cheese, shrimp, half of the crab, the garlic, garlic powder, chili powder, Old Bay, black pepper, Cajun seasoning, cayenne (if using), onion powder, sazón, and paprika. Mix thoroughly.

5   Transfer the dip to a baking dish and create a pocket in the middle. Add the remaining crab to the pocket, then cover the surrounding dip with the mozzarella.

6   Bake for 20 to 25 minutes, until the cheese is beginning to brown. Sprinkle with paprika and parsley and enjoy with tortilla chips!

Pro Tips

1   Shrimp cook very quickly! Be careful not to overcook.

2   This dip can be prepared through step 5 up to 2 days in advance and refrigerated until you wish to bake!

FRIED LOADED BAKED POTATO BALLS

15 TO 20 POTATO BALLS	PREP: 40 MINUTES	COOK: 25 MINUTES

INGREDIENTS

4 to 5 medium russet potatoes, peeled and cut into 2-inch chunks

Salt

8 to 12 tablespoons unsalted butter, melted

½ cup milk

½ cup sour cream

3 garlic cloves, minced

2 teaspoons garlic powder

2 teaspoons Italian seasoning

1 teaspoon black pepper

1 teaspoon smoked paprika

¼ cup shredded cheddar

5 strips bacon, cooked and chopped

1 teaspoon chopped chives

Neutral oil, for frying

2 cups breadcrumbs

¾ cup grated Romano

1 cup all-purpose flour

3 to 4 large eggs, beaten

Potatoes are good pretty much any way you make them! Turn them into a soup or fries, bake them or mash them. And this recipe is so fun to make. I took mashed potatoes and essentially turned them into fries, with a soft, creamy center. Feel free to make them as big or as small as you'd like! Then pair them with Easy Buttermilk Ranch (page 239).

1   Place the potatoes in a pot, cover with water, lightly salt, and bring to a boil.

2   Strain and mash lightly. Add the butter, milk, and sour cream. Mix thoroughly.

3   Stir in the garlic, garlic powder, Italian seasoning, pepper, paprika, and 1 teaspoon salt. Then add the cheddar, bacon, and chives. Taste the potatoes—if they're missing anything, now is the time to season them!

4   Transfer to the refrigerator to cool completely, for at least 2 to 3 hours (see Pro Tip).

5   Heat about 3 cups of oil to 350°F in a medium pot.

6   Mix the breadcrumbs and Romano in a wide shallow bowl. Add the flour to a separate shallow bowl. Whisk the eggs in a third shallow bowl.

7   Form the mashed potato mixture into balls, using about ¼ cup for each. Dip the balls into the flour, then the eggs, and then coat thoroughly with the breadcrumb mixture.

8   Fry until golden brown and warmed through, 3 to 4 minutes. Lightly sprinkle with salt to taste and serve immediately.

Pro Tip

The potatoes must be chilled completely so they'll stay intact when frying.

SOUTHWEST CHICKEN DIP
WITH EGGROLL CHIPS

5 TO 6 SERVINGS	PREP: 35 MINUTES	COOK: 25 MINUTES

INGREDIENTS

8 ounces cream cheese, softened

6 ounces shredded cheddar

1 tablespoon garlic paste

1½ teaspoons sazón

1 teaspoon black pepper

1 teaspoon garlic powder

1 teaspoon smoked paprika

½ teaspoon cayenne (optional)

½ rotisserie chicken, shredded
  (about 3 cups; see Pro Tip)

One 15-ounce can black beans,
  drained

One 15-ounce can corn, drained

One 10-ounce can diced tomatoes and
  green chiles

One 4-ounce can diced green chiles

½ cup pickled jalapeños, diced

6 ounces shredded Colby Jack

Chopped green onions

Sliced jalapeños (optional)

Neutral oil, for frying

10 to 12 wonton wrappers,
  halved diagonally

This recipe has all the delicious flavors of a southwest chicken egg roll, turned into an amazing dip! Dips are so versatile; they're a staple in the appetizer game, and you can add almost anything you want (plus a little cheese), and you're good to go! This recipe is great if you fry up some wonton wrappers in place of tortilla chips.

1   Preheat the oven to 350°F.

2   Mix the cream cheese, cheddar, garlic paste, sazón, black pepper. garlic powder, paprika, and cayenne. Fold in the chicken, beans, corn, tomatoes, chiles, and jalapeños.

3   Spread the mixture evenly into a medium cast-iron skillet. Top with the Colby Jack and bake for 15 to 20 minutes, until all the cheese on top has melted. Broil for 60 seconds to ensure a bubbly brown top. Top with green onions and jalapeños, if desired.

4   Heat about 2 cups of frying oil to 350°F in a medium pot. Add in the wonton wrappers and fry until lightly golden brown, 1 to 2 minutes. Lightly salt immediately. Enjoy with the dip!

Pro Tip

If you prefer white meat, the meat from two breasts should suffice. But the dark meat will add amazing flavor!

GARLIC BUTTER WHITE WINE SCALLOPS

3 TO 4 SERVINGS	PREP: 15 MINUTES	COOK: 15 MINUTES

INGREDIENTS

2 tablespoons olive oil

1 pound scallops, patted dry

½ teaspoon garlic powder

1 teaspoon white pepper

½ teaspoon onion powder

¼ teaspoon smoked paprika

¼ teaspoon salt

3 tablespoons unsalted butter

½ small shallot, minced

4 garlic cloves, minced

Juice of 1 lemon

¼ cup white wine

1 teaspoon chopped fresh parsley, plus more for serving

½ teaspoon red pepper flakes

Freshly grated Parmesan (optional)

If I could only use three words to describe this recipe, they would be fresh, crisp, and tasty. The light sauce really brings out the flavor of the scallops. While this recipe is made to be an appetizer, it's also a perfect addition to any meal; you can even double or triple the recipe and make it the main attraction. If you're not a fan of scallops, you can sub in shrimp and still end up with a hit.

1   Heat the olive oil in a medium pan over medium-high heat.

2   Season the scallops on both sides with garlic powder, white pepper, onion powder, paprika, and salt.

3   Add the scallops to the hot pan. Sear on one side for 1 to 2 minutes, then flip. Sear the other side for another 1 to 2 minutes. Remove the scallops from the pan.

4   Turn the heat to medium and add the butter and shallot. Cook until fragrant, 2 to 3 minutes, then add the garlic (see Pro Tip) and cook until lightly browned and toasted, 1 to 2 minutes.

5   Add the lemon juice, wine, parsley, and red pepper flakes.

6   Cook until the alcohol has evaporated and the sauce has slightly thickened, 1 to 2 minutes, and add the scallops back to the pan. Allow the flavors to marinate for another minute or so, then remove from heat.

7   Garnish with parsley and Parmesan, if desired. Enjoy!

Pro Tip

Make sure the pan has reduced to medium heat before adding the garlic. It can burn very quickly!

AIR-FRIED BLACKENED CHICKEN TENDERS WITH BUTTERMILK RANCH

3 SERVINGS	PREP: 20 MINUTES	COOK: 30 MINUTES

INGREDIENTS

1 pound chicken tenders

1 tablespoon olive oil

1 teaspoon black pepper

1 teaspoon chili powder

1 teaspoon garlic powder

1 teaspoon onion powder

1 teaspoon dried oregano

1 teaspoon salt

Chopped fresh parsley

1 batch Easy Buttermilk Ranch
(page 239)

I am a chicken tender connoisseur. I'm the person who orders chicken tenders at every restaurant if I don't know what else to get! I mean, you can hardly mess tenders up. They're delicious with any dipping sauce, and you're always satisfied! This air-fryer recipe is perfect, especially if you like to do minimal cleanup!

1   In a large bowl, combine the chicken, olive oil, black pepper, chili powder, garlic powder, onion powder, oregano, and salt. Thoroughly mix the seasoning into the chicken, then transfer to the fridge to chill for at least 15 minutes.

2   Preheat the air fryer to 375°F.

3   Place the chicken in the air fryer and cook until blackened and slightly crispy, 14 to 17 minutes (see Pro Tip).

4   Garnish with parsley, serve with the ranch, and enjoy!

Pro Tip

Be careful not to overcrowd the air fryer, as this will result in longer cook times and less-crispy tenders. Cook in batches if needed.

PHILLY CHEESESTEAK EGG ROLLS
WITH HONEY-SRIRACHA GLAZE

6 TO 8 SERVINGS	PREP: 10 MINUTES	COOK: 55 MINUTES

INGREDIENTS

2 tablespoons unsalted butter

¼ cup finely diced green bell pepper

¼ cup finely diced red bell pepper

¼ cup finely diced yellow onion

1 pound ribeye steak, shaved

2 teaspoons garlic powder

1 teaspoon black pepper

1 teaspoon chili powder

1 teaspoon onion powder

1 teaspoon salt

1 cup shredded mozzarella

Neutral oil, for frying

8 egg roll wrappers

8 provolone slices, halved

Honey-Sriracha Glaze

½ cup honey

2 tablespoons sriracha

1 teaspoon red pepper flakes

If I had to choose one egg roll to eat for the rest of my life, this would be it. I mean no disrespect to Philadelphia, but if you're from Philly, try these out and let me know if I have the approval! Paired with a sweet and spicy dipping sauce, these egg rolls are sure to make it to the next party table.

1   To a medium pan over medium heat, add the butter, bell peppers, and onion. Sauté until tender, 4 to 5 minutes.

2   Add the steak, garlic powder, black pepper, chili powder, onion powder, and salt. Cook until well done, 5 to 7 minutes, then slowly mix in the mozzarella. Remove from the heat and let cool for 2 to 3 minutes.

3   Fill a cast-iron skillet about halfway with oil and heat to 375°F.

4   Lay out an egg roll wrapper so one of the points is facing toward you. Set out a small bowl of water.

5   Place half a provolone slice onto the wrapper, then add 2 to 3 tablespoons of the meat mixture on top.

6   Dip your fingertips into the water bowl. Fold the bottom corner of the wrapper over the mixture, then fold in the right and left sides. Roll the egg roll tightly from the bottom up, then fold the top point over the roll. Repeat steps 4 through 6 with the remaining wrappers and filling.

7   Place the egg rolls in the refrigerator for about 5 minutes to firm up a bit.

8   **Make the glaze:** In a small bowl, mix the honey, sriracha, and red pepper flakes.

9   Add the egg rolls to the oil, in batches if necessary, and fry until golden brown, 2 to 3 minutes. Transfer to a paper towel to drain, then immediately drizzle with the glaze.

HOMEMADE GUACAMOLE & TORTILLA CHIPS

4 TO 5 SERVINGS | PREP: 20 MINUTES | COOK: 45 MINUTES

INGREDIENTS

Guacamole

3 medium avocados, halved, peeled, and pitted

2 Roma tomatoes, seeded and diced

½ small red onion, diced

Juice of 1 lime

¼ cup chopped fresh cilantro

1 to 2 jalapeños, diced (optional)

½ teaspoon black pepper

½ teaspoon salt

Tortilla Chips

Neutral oil, for frying

15 small corn tortillas, quartered

Salt

My fiancée and I recently discovered a love for avocados. Ever hear the saying, "Your taste buds change every seven years"? Well, we are living proof! There's just something blissful about fresh avocado or homemade guacamole with tortilla chips. Add this to any dish that requires guacamole, and you'll never buy store-bought again!

1 **Make the guacamole:** In a large bowl, mash the avocados. Fold in the tomatoes, onion, lime juice, cilantro, jalapeños (if using), black pepper, and salt. Mix well.

2 **Make the tortilla chips:** Heat about 2 cups of oil to 375°F in a medium pot.

3 Drop 4 tortilla pieces at a time into the oil. Fry until crispy and lightly golden brown, stirring to avoid burning, 1 to 2 minutes. Transfer to a paper towel-lined plate to drain and immediately sprinkle with salt.

4 Enjoy the guacamole at room temperature or cover tightly with plastic wrap (see Pro Tip) and set in the fridge to cool for at least 30 minutes.

Pro Tip

Place the plastic wrap directly on top of the guacamole and not around the bowl. This will prevent the guacamole from browning!

SPICY CRAB RANGOONS

| 25 RANGOONS | PREP: 40 MINUTES | COOK: 15 MINUTES |

INGREDIENTS

Neutral oil, for frying

10 to 12 ounces imitation crab meat (sticks or chunks)

6 ounces cream cheese, softened

2 green onions, sliced (about ¼ cup)

1 tablespoon lemon juice

2 tablespoon sriracha

1 teaspoon garlic powder

1 teaspoon onion powder

1 teaspoon white pepper

25 wonton wrappers

Crab rangoons are one of the most delicious Chinese takeout dishes, but sometimes they're just too sweet for me. So how do we combat sweetness? Add spice! This twist on a traditional crab rangoon has a little kick and is definitely worth checking out. Pair with the honey-sriracha glaze on page 74!

1 Heat about 2½ cups of oil to 375°F in a medium pot.

2 To a large bowl, add the crab and use a spoon to break it into small pieces.

3 Gently fold in the cream cheese until all of the crab is covered. Stir in the green onions, lemon juice, sriracha, garlic powder, onion powder, and pepper.

4 Lay out a wonton wrapper and add 1 tablespoon of filling to the center. Brush the edges lightly with water, then bring the opposite corners to touch to form a point at the top. Press firmly to seal on every side.

5 Fry, in batches if needed, until crispy and golden brown, about 2 minutes. Let cool and enjoy.

AIR-FRIED CHICKEN WINGS

10 TO 12 WINGS	PREP: 10 MINUTES	COOK: 25 MINUTES

INGREDIENTS

1 pound chicken wings (drums and flats)

1 tablespoon olive oil

2 teaspoons cornstarch

1 teaspoon black pepper

1 teaspoon chili powder

1 teaspoon garlic powder

1 teaspoon onion powder

1 teaspoon oregano

¼ teaspoon salt

I love wings, and I love them crispy. And this recipe here is one of my favorites. Throw these in the air fryer, make a quick side dish (see pages 164 to 185), and dinner is served in under 20 minutes. Be careful—these wings are addicting!

1   Preheat the air fryer to 375°F.

2   In a large bowl, combine the chicken wings, olive oil, cornstarch, pepper, chili powder, garlic powder, onion powder, oregano, and salt.

3   Let sit for about 5 minutes (see Pro Tip 1), then add to the air fryer.

4   Add the wings to the air fryer and cook on one side for 10 to 12 minutes (see Pro Tip 2). Flip and cook for another 10 to 12 minutes, until extra crispy. Remove from the air fryer and enjoy while hot!

Pro Tips

1   Letting the wings sit will help them achieve an extra crispy outer layer.

2   If you don't have an air fryer, fry the wings in a neutral oil for 6 to 8 minutes.

LOADED CRAWFISH POTATO SKINS

4 TO 5 SERVINGS	PREP: 40 MINUTES	COOK: 90 MINUTES

INGREDIENTS

4 medium russet potatoes

2 tablespoons olive oil

Salt

1 tablespoon butter

1 pound crawfish tail meat

1 teaspoon Old Bay seasoning

½ teaspoon black pepper

½ teaspoon garlic powder

¼ teaspoon cayenne

½ cup heavy cream

4 to 5 ounces shredded Colby Jack

4 strips bacon, cooked and diced

¼ cup diced green onions

Sour cream

This is an amazing way to enjoy a potato. I think it's funny that most people will eat the insides of a baked potato but not the skin. But when eating loaded potato skins, they eat the whole potato—and you'll want to do that with this recipe, too. Substitute the crawfish for shrimp or lobster for a great alternative!

1 Preheat the oven to 400°F. Lightly coat the outsides of the potatoes with olive oil and salt. Wrap in foil and bake for about 1 hour, until fork-tender. Let cool.

2 Halve the potatoes lengthwise, then scoop out the flesh, leaving ¼ inch or more of the flesh (set aside for another use).

3 Heat the butter in a medium pan over medium heat. Add the crawfish tails, Old Bay, black pepper, garlic powder, and cayenne. Cook until the tails begin to shrink slightly, 2 to 3 minutes.

4 Stir in the heavy cream, then bring to a simmer until thickened, 3 to 4 minutes. Remove from the heat.

5 Fill each potato skin with the crawfish filling, then add the cheese. Top with bacon, then bake for about 10 minutes, until the cheese has melted.

6 Garnish with fresh green onion and sour cream. Enjoy!

BOURBON-GLAZED FRIED SALMON NUGGETS

3 TO 4 SERVINGS	PREP: 45 MINUTES	COOK: 35 MINUTES

INGREDIENTS

1½ pounds skinless salmon, cut into 1- to 2-inch cubes

1 cup buttermilk

½ cup hot sauce

Neutral oil, for frying

Flour Coating

2 cups all-purpose flour

1 tablespoon garlic powder

1 tablespoon lemon pepper

1 tablespoon onion powder

1 tablespoon smoked paprika

1 teaspoon black pepper

1 teaspoon cayenne

Bourbon Glaze

½ cup brown sugar

¼ cup apple cider vinegar

¼ cup honey

Juice of ½ orange

2 tablespoons soy sauce

1 garlic clove, minced

1 teaspoon minced ginger

¾ cup bourbon

Bourbon glaze is one of the most flavorful sauces out there, and no, it doesn't get you drunk. (Unless you're pouring a couple glasses on the side when making this recipe—nobody's judging!) Fried salmon is one of those things you don't see too often, but as soon as you try it, I promise you'll be hooked. These nuggets are perfect for dipping in spicy ranch.

1   In a large bowl, combine the salmon, buttermilk, and hot sauce. Place in the refrigerator and let marinate for at least 30 minutes.

2   **Make the coating:** In a large bowl, combine the flour, garlic powder, lemon pepper, onion powder, paprika, black pepper, and cayenne. Mix well.

3   **Make the glaze:** In a medium saucepan over low heat, combine the brown sugar, vinegar, honey, orange juice, soy sauce, garlic, and ginger. Bring to a simmer.

4   Add the bourbon and cook out the alcohol, 5 to 8 minutes. The sauce should begin to thicken slightly, enough to coat the back of a spoon. Remove from the heat and let cool.

5   Heat 2 to 3 cups of oil to 375°F in a medium pot.

6   Add the salmon, a few pieces at a time, to the flour mixture until all pieces are thoroughly coated and you can no longer see the salmon underneath.

7   Add the salmon to the oil and fry, in batches if needed, until golden brown, 5 to 7 minutes. Transfer to a paper towel-lined plate.

8   While the salmon is still hot, lightly toss in a bowl, coating the nuggets with the glaze. Enjoy!

CHEESY SHRIMP EMPANADAS

10 EMPANADAS	PREP: 25 MINUTES	COOK: 25 MINUTES

INGREDIENTS

Neutral oil, for frying

1 pound medium raw shrimp, shelled, deveined, and chopped

1 teaspoon garlic powder

1 teaspoon onion powder

1 teaspoon black pepper

1 teaspoon sazón

2 teaspoons olive oil

¼ cup tomato sauce

¼ cup chopped fresh cilantro

10 frozen empanada discos (dough), thawed

1 cup shredded cheddar

Empanadas are a true piece of my childhood. Growing up, my mother always made empanadas with a side of Arroz con Gandules (page 183). The only issue is that she never made enough! The best way to enjoy this dish is to eat the hot empanada fresh out of the oil, wrapped in a paper towel. Trust me.

1   Preheat 2 inches of frying oil to 375°F in a deep medium pan.

2   In a large bowl, combine the shrimp, garlic powder, onion powder, black pepper, and sazón.

3   Heat the olive oil in a medium pan over medium heat, then add the shrimp. Cook until the shrimp begin to shrink slightly, 3 to 4 minutes, then stir in the tomato sauce and cilantro. Remove from the heat.

4   Lay out your empanada discos and place 1 to 2 tablespoons of the shrimp filling into the middle of each empanada. Sprinkle 1 to 2 tablespoons of cheese on top of the shrimp filling.

5   Fold the dough in half over the filling and use a fork to crimp the edges closed.

6   Place the empanadas into the frying oil and fry until the dough begins to bubble up, 1 to 2 minutes per side. Let cool briefly before eating. Enjoy!

CRAB CAKE STUFFED CHEDDAR BISCUITS

8 BISCUITS	PREP: 45 MINUTES	COOK: 20 MINUTES

INGREDIENTS

Crab Cakes

8 ounces lump crab meat

1½ tablespoons mayonnaise

2 teaspoons yellow mustard

2 teaspoons Worcestershire sauce

1½ teaspoons garlic powder

1 teaspoon Cajun seasoning

1 teaspoon onion powder

1 teaspoon chili powder

½ teaspoon sazón

¼ teaspoon black pepper

¼ to ½ cup panko breadcrumbs

1 tablespoon olive oil

Biscuits

4 cups buttermilk biscuit mix,
   such as Bisquick

2 cups shredded cheddar

2 teaspoons garlic powder, divided

1½ teaspoons dried oregano

½ teaspoon salt

1⅓ cups milk

16 tablespoons butter

Chopped fresh parsley

2 lemons, quartered

This recipe is so special to me, because it essentially kicked off where I am now. One night, my now-fiancée and I were having a couple drinks, eating crab cakes and cheddar biscuits. She suggested that I try to stuff one of the crab cakes into a biscuit, and the rest was history. This signature recipe of mine will forever be special!

1   Preheat the oven to 400°F. Line two baking sheets with parchment paper.

2   **Make the crab cakes:** In a large bowl, combine the crab, mayonnaise, mustard, Worcestershire sauce, garlic powder, Cajun seasoning, onion powder, chili powder, sazón, and black pepper. Slowly add ¼ cup breadcrumbs until the mixture is no longer wet and will hold a firm shape. (Add more breadcrumbs if the mixture is still too wet.)

3   Press the mixture into eight small patties, about 2 inches in diameter. Place in the refrigerator for 5 to 10 minutes to allow them to firm up.

4   Heat a large skillet over medium heat, then add the olive oil. Add the crab cakes and cook until golden brown on each side, 2 to 3 minutes per side. Remove from the heat and set aside to cool.

5   **Make the biscuits:** In a large bowl, combine the biscuit mix, cheddar, 1 teaspoon of garlic powder, the oregano, and salt. Mix well, then add the milk and stir to combine. (The mixture will be very sticky; use gloves if you'd like, to keep it from sticking to your hands.)

6   In one hand, place enough biscuit dough (2 to 3 tablespoons) to cover the bottom of one crab cake. Place the crab cake on top of the dough, then place another 2 to 3 tablespoons of dough on the top of the crab cake. Pinch the sides to seal, adding small amounts of dough as needed. Repeat with the remaining crab cakes and biscuit dough.

7   Place the stuffed biscuits onto the baking sheets, then bake for 10 to 12 minutes, until the biscuits are golden brown and the cheddar flakes are light brown.

8   While the biscuits are cooking, mix the butter, parsley, and the remaining teaspoon of garlic powder in a small bowl. Microwave for 30 seconds to melt the butter.

9   Remove the biscuits from the oven and immediately brush the warm butter on top. Garnish with the lemon quarters. Enjoy!

LUNCH

Lunch: the meal between breakfast and dinner, the meal if you haven't eaten breakfast, the meal that might make you skip dinner, all in one. Lunch is one of those meals that you either commit to daily or you skip completely. Sometimes you may have a full sit-down meal, or you might munch on a quick grab-and-go meal because you're in a time crunch.

The fondest memories I have of lunchtime are of me staring down the clock in school, waiting for the bell to ring to send us to lunch each day. Whether you packed your own lunch or ate whatever the cafeteria was serving, after being hungry all morning in class, a moment to sit down and eat some food felt like the best thing in the world! This is one of the reasons I started taking a moment to truly enjoy lunchtime. When I was growing up, my mom would sometimes take me and my brothers out to lunch on Saturdays. We would all get in the car, go eat lunch somewhere, and then come home and take a nap!

In this chapter, you'll find traditional and non-traditional takes on lunch. Of course we have to have some sandwiches—what's better than a delicious, hearty sandwich? If you're not a fan of sandwiches, what about tacos? Stuffed salmon? Slow-cooked chili? Don't worry—whatever your midday lunch cravings are, there is something in here for you!

BUFFALO-RANCH GRILLED CHICKEN SANDWICHES

4 TO 5 SERVINGS	PREP: 25 MINUTES	COOK: 15 MINUTES

INGREDIENTS

2 pounds chicken breast, cut into 6-ounce portions (see Pro Tip)

1 cup Italian dressing

1½ teaspoons garlic powder

1½ teaspoons dried oregano

1 teaspoon chili powder

½ teaspoon black pepper

Pepper Jack slices

4 to 5 brioche sandwich buns, sliced horizontally

¼ cup Easy Buttermilk Ranch (page 239)

Lettuce leaves

Tomato slices

Buffalo Sauce

1 cup hot sauce

4 tablespoons butter, melted

1 tablespoon garlic paste

Is it just me or do Buffalo and ranch together always sound like a green light? This recipe was inspired by a favorite appetizer of mine, Buffalo-ranch chicken dip, so I decided to turn it into a sandwich! Hop on the grill, add whatever toppings you'd like, and dig in!

1 In a large bowl, combine the chicken, Italian dressing, garlic powder, dried oregano, chili powder, and black pepper. Cover and allow the chicken to marinate in the refrigerator for at least 1 hour.

2 Fire up your grill or flat top griddle and allow the charcoal to get hot (350 to 400°F).

3 **Make the Buffalo sauce:** In a small bowl, combine the hot sauce, melted butter, and garlic paste.

4 Place your chicken on the grill and cook until nicely seared, at least 4 minutes per side. Baste each side lightly with the Buffalo sauce.

5 Transfer the chicken to a cooler spot on the grill, top with the cheese, and allow the cheese to melt, 2 to 3 minutes.

6 Meanwhile, place the buns on the grill, cut side down, until lightly toasted, 1 to 2 minutes.

7 Spread a thin layer of ranch onto the bottom bun, dress with lettuce and tomato, and add the chicken. Top with more ranch and add your top bun. Enjoy!

Pro Tip

It is important to cut the chicken into even portions. This will ensure that each piece of chicken is cooked evenly and fully through.

STEAK QUESADILLA

1 TO 2 SERVINGS	PREP: 12 MINUTES	COOK: 20 MINUTES

INGREDIENTS

1 pound ribeye steak

1 teaspoon chili powder

1 teaspoon garlic powder

1 teaspoon onion powder

1 teaspoon black pepper

½ teaspoon ground cumin

½ teaspoon salt (optional)

2 teaspoons olive oil

2 large flour tortillas

10 to 12 ounces shredded
   Oaxaca cheese

To Serve

Sour cream

Salsa

Guacamole (see page 77)

Lime wedges

Remember that guacamole recipe from page 77? You're gonna want to make that along with this delicious steak quesadilla. Quesadillas and I have a long history; in high school, I worked at a restaurant, and while it was a BBQ restaurant, they had lots of tortillas around, so I made quesadillas at least twice a week. Fill them with whatever you want, and don't forget extra sour cream!

1   Place the steak in the freezer for about 15 minutes (see Pro Tip 1). Remove from the freezer and thinly slice.

2   Season the steak with chili powder, garlic powder, onion powder, black pepper, cumin, and salt, if using.

3   Heat the oil in a large pan over medium-high heat.

4   Add the steak and cook until medium-well and nicely seared, 3 to 5 minutes (see Pro Tip 2).

5   Remove the steak from the pan. Reduce the heat to medium-low and add the tortilla. Spread half of the cheese over the entire tortilla, then add your steak.

6   Top with the other half of the cheese, add on another tortilla, then use a spatula to flip and press down (see Pro Tip 3).

7   Cook until the cheese is melted and the tortilla shell is crispy, about 2 minutes.

8   Slice immediately and garnish with sour cream, salsa, and guacamole. Serve with lime wedges. Enjoy!

Pro Tips

1   Freezing the steak will help you achieve thin slices more easily.

2   If you prefer well-done steak, cook for a few more minutes.

3   If your tortilla is falling apart, allow the second tortilla to slightly adhere to the other tortilla by allowing the cheese to melt for 1 to 2 minutes before flipping.

COBB SALAD
WITH CHIPOTLE RANCH

3 TO 4 SERVINGS	PREP: 20 MINUTES	COOK: 15 MINUTES

INGREDIENTS

3 strips thick-cut bacon

½ pound chicken breast

1 teaspoon chili powder

1 teaspoon dried dill

1 teaspoon garlic powder

1 teaspoon onion powder

1 teaspoon black pepper

1 romaine heart, chopped

1 medium cucumber, diced

2 hard-boiled eggs, peeled and diced

15 cherry tomatoes, halved

½ small red onion, diced

¼ cup crumbled feta

Chipotle Ranch

1 cup Easy Buttermilk Ranch
(page 239)

2 tablespoons diced chipotle peppers
in adobo sauce

Salads are one of the most appetizing things you can eat, in my opinion. There are literally no rules about what can go into your salad. Boiled eggs? Bacon bits? Roasted peppers? Ten different cheeses? It doesn't matter—it's all going to be good once you mix it together!

1 **Make the chipotle ranch:** In a small bowl, combine the ranch and chipotles. Transfer to the refrigerator to chill.

2 Heat a medium pan over medium heat and add the bacon. Cook until crispy, a few minutes per side, then remove from the pan. Keep the bacon grease in the pan.

3 In a large bowl, season the chicken with chili powder, dill, garlic powder, onion powder, and black pepper.

4 Add the chicken to the pan and cook until cooked through, flipping halfway through, 7 to 8 minutes. Remove the chicken from the pan and cut into cubes.

5 **Assemble the salad:** In a large bowl, mix the lettuce, cucumber, eggs, tomatoes, onion, feta, and bacon. Add the chicken, top the salad with chipotle ranch, and enjoy!

CAJUN BUTTER SEAFOOD BOIL PAN

4 TO 5 SERVINGS	PREP: 15 MINUTES	COOK: 20 MINUTES

INGREDIENTS

2 pounds snow crab legs

3 bay leaves

1 tablespoon chili powder

1 tablespoon garlic powder

1 tablespoon onion powder

1 tablespoon paprika

1½ teaspoons black pepper

1 teaspoon cayenne

1 medium orange, halved

2 lemons, halved

2 ears of corn, cut crosswise into 3-inch pieces

6 medium red potatoes

2 large smoked sausage links

1 pound jumbo shell-on shrimp

4 large eggs, hard-boiled and peeled

Chopped fresh parsley

Cajun Butter

16 tablespoons unsalted butter

1½ tablespoons garlic paste

1 tablespoon chopped fresh parsley

2½ teaspoons onion powder

2½ teaspoons paprika

1 to 2 teaspoons cayenne

2 teaspoons black pepper

1 teaspoon chili powder

Juice of 1 lemon

Skip the expensive boil-in-a-bag restaurants and make your own seafood boil, ten times better and right at home! My family loves seafood, so on Christmas a few years back, we decided to fill our entire table with seafood—snow crab legs, king crab legs, jumbo shrimp, mussels—plus potatoes, boiled eggs, sausage, and corn. It's one of my favorite Christmas memories; is there a better way to enjoy the holidays?

1   Place the crab legs in a large pot, then fill with just enough water to cover. Remove the crab, then bring the water to a boil.

2   Season the water with bay leaves, chili powder, garlic powder, onion powder, paprika, black pepper, and cayenne. Squeeze in the juice from the orange and lemons, then add them in as well.

3   When the water has reached a rolling boil, add the potatoes and sausage. Cook until the potatoes are tender, 10 to 12 minutes.

4   Add the corn and cook until slightly tender, another 4 to 5 minutes. Transfer the corn, potatoes, and sausage to a large pan.

5   Add the crab legs to the pot and cook for about 3 minutes. Remove the crab, then add the shrimp. Allow the shrimp to cook thoroughly, 3 to 4 minutes, then transfer to the pan. Add the eggs to the pan.

6   **Make the Cajun butter:** To a microwave-safe dish, add the butter, garlic paste, parsley, onion powder, paprika, cayenne, black pepper, chili powder, and lemon juice. Microwave in 15-second increments until the butter has just begun to melt and is still creamy.

7   Remove from the microwave and mix well. Pour the butter (save some to dip your cracked crab legs in!) into the bowl and toss to combine.

8   Garnish with fresh parsley. Enjoy!

GRILLED LEMON-HERB CHICKEN
WITH STRING BEANS

6 SERVINGS	PREP: 15 MINUTES	COOK: 30 MINUTES

INGREDIENTS

2 tablespoons olive oil, divided

2 pounds chicken breast, sliced into thin cutlets

1½ tablespoons chili powder, divided

1½ tablespoons garlic powder, divided

1½ tablespoons onion powder, divided

2 teaspoons black pepper

1 teaspoon salt

1 pound string beans, trimmed

Juice of 1 lemon

1 lemon, thinly sliced

Paprika

One of the healthier recipes in this book, this dish is a go-to of mine when I feel like eating on the lighter side. But that doesn't mean that it has to lack in flavor! Fire up the grill, season your chicken well, and enjoy this quick meal.

1   Place charcoal into a grill, light, and heat until all of the charcoal has been covered with ash and is a grayish-white color, about 15 minutes (see Pro Tip).

2   Place a cast-iron skillet on the grill over direct heat. Cover the bottom of the pan with 1 tablespoon of olive oil and warm, 10 to 15 minutes.

3   While the skillet is heating, season the chicken with 1 tablespoon each of olive oil, chili powder, garlic powder, onion powder, and black pepper, and the salt.

4   Place the chicken onto direct heat on the grill, and cook until nicely charred, flipping once, 4 to 5 minutes per side.

5   After flipping the chicken, add the string beans to the skillet and season with the remaining chili powder, garlic powder, and onion powder. Cook until crisp-tender, 3 to 5 minutes, then add the lemon juice and stir.

6   Place the chicken on top of the string beans, then place the lemon slices on top. Close the grill and allow the flavors to combine for 2 to 3 minutes. Sprinkle with paprika and enjoy!

Pro Tip

You can also use a gas grill or even a skillet on the stovetop for this recipe. But you'll achieve the best results and flavor with a charcoal grill!

HOT HONEY MUSTARD FRIED SHRIMP

3 TO 4 SERVINGS	PREP: 15 MINUTES	COOK: 20 MINUTES

INGREDIENTS

Shrimp

Neutral oil, for frying

1½ pounds jumbo shrimp, peeled and deveined

2 large eggs

¼ cup hot sauce

¼ cup yellow mustard

2 cups all-purpose flour

1 tablespoon garlic powder

1 tablespoon onion powder

1 tablespoon paprika

1 tablespoon black pepper

1 to 2 teaspoons salt

Sliced green onions

Hot Honey Mustard

¼ cup honey

¼ cup mayonnaise

¼ cup Dijon mustard

1 teaspoon apple cider vinegar

½ teaspoon hot sauce

¼ teaspoon cayenne

Fried shrimp is one of my uncle's specialties. Every year when he visits, everybody requests that he make his famous fried shrimp. His trick is to use a small pot to fry only a few shrimp at a time. I hope my recipe is at least half as good as his!

1 Preheat about 3 cups of frying oil to 375°F in a medium pot.

2 **Make the honey mustard:** In a small bowl, combine the honey, mayonnaise, mustard, vinegar, hot sauce, and cayenne. (If you prefer a spicier sauce, increase the amount of cayenne.)

3 **Make the shrimp:** In a large bowl, combine the shrimp, eggs, hot sauce, and mustard.

4 In another bowl, combine the flour, garlic powder, onion powder, paprika, pepper, and salt to taste.

5 Add your shrimp to the flour and coat evenly and thoroughly, to ensure maximum crispiness.

6 Add the shrimp to the oil and fry until golden brown and crispy, 2 to 3 minutes. (For crunchier shrimp, fry for 4 to 5 minutes.)

7 Toss the shrimp in the honey mustard sauce or serve the sauce on the side. Top with green onions. Enjoy!

TURKEY & BEAN CHILI

4 TO 5 SERVINGS	PREP: 15 MINUTES	COOK: 75 MINUTES

INGREDIENTS

1 tablespoon vegetable oil

½ cup diced yellow onion

½ cup diced green bell pepper

2 pounds ground turkey

One 28-ounce can crushed tomatoes

¼ cup Worcestershire sauce

2 tablespoons tomato paste

3 teaspoons garlic powder

3 teaspoons onion powder

2 teaspoons chili powder

2 teaspoons black pepper

1 teaspoon ground cumin

1 teaspoon salt

One 16-ounce can dark red
kidney beans

One 16-ounce can light red
kidney beans

To Serve

Sour cream

Shredded cheddar

Chopped chives

I know many people think ground turkey is flavorless, bland, and dry. But when I was growing up, ground turkey was the only ground meat we used. Not sure if it was because of cost, personal preference, or flavor, but it always tasted good! I have fond memories of my mother making a pot of chili and frying up some chicken tenders to go on the side. I'm not sure why she did that, but it goes well together!

1   To a medium pot over medium heat, add the oil, onion, and bell pepper. Cook until the vegetables are tender, 3 to 4 minutes.

2   Add the turkey and cook until mostly cooked through, breaking it up into small pieces, 6 to 7 minutes.

3   Add the crushed tomatoes, Worcestershire sauce, and tomato paste. Stir in the garlic powder, onion powder, chili powder, black pepper, cumin, and salt.

4   Cover the pot and allow the chili to simmer over low heat for at least 45 minutes, stirring occasionally (see Pro Tip).

5   Stir in the beans and taste the chili. Adjust the seasoning to taste.

6   Garnish with sour cream, cheddar, and chives, the Eatwitzo way. Enjoy!

Pro Tip

You can cook the chili for longer, if preferred. An hour is ideal!

BEEF & BROCCOLI FRIED RICE

2 TO 3 SERVINGS	PREP: 15 MINUTES	COOK: 25 MINUTES

INGREDIENTS

Beef & Broccoli
1 tablespoon vegetable oil
1 pound sirloin steak, thinly sliced
1 teaspoon chili powder
1 tablespoon cornstarch
1 teaspoon garlic powder
1 teaspoon onion powder
1 teaspoon black pepper
½ teaspoon salt
2 cups broccoli florets

Sauce
2 tablespoons soy sauce
1 tablespoon brown sugar
1½ teaspoons garlic paste
1 teaspoon sesame oil

Fried Rice
1 tablespoon unsalted butter
½ cup frozen mixed vegetables
2 large eggs
3 cups cooked, day-old white rice
¼ to ½ cup soy sauce
1 tablespoon oyster sauce
1 teaspoon sesame oil
Sesame seeds

This is for sure a top-five Chinese takeout dish! Beef and broccoli was one of my mother's favorites when I was growing up, and it eventually became one of mine as well. My ideal takeout meal: beef and broccoli, white rice, a couple egg rolls, and a grape soda, The savory and tender beef paired with the crunchy, flavorful broccoli is amazing. Plus, fried rice is easier than you think to make at home!

1 **Make the beef and broccoli:** Heat the vegetable oil in a large pan or wok over medium-high heat.

2 In a large bowl, combine the steak, chili powder, cornstarch, garlic powder, onion powder, pepper, and salt. Mix well, then add the steak to the pan.

3 Cook to medium-well or well done, 5 to 7 minutes. Remove from the pan and set aside.

4 Reduce the heat to medium, then add the broccoli to the pan. Cook until slightly charred and fragrant, 3 to 4 minutes. Remove from the pan.

5 **Make the sauce:** To the same pan, add the soy sauce, sugar, garlic paste, and sesame oil. Mix and let come to a low simmer until thickened, 2 to 3 minutes. Set aside.

6 **Make the fried rice:** Melt the butter in another large pan or wok over medium-high heat.

7 Add the frozen vegetables and warm them slightly, 2 to 3 minutes (see Pro Tip).

8 Add the eggs to the pan and scramble them, mixing with the vegetables. Add the rice, followed by the soy sauce to taste, oyster sauce, and sesame oil. Toss the rice thoroughly until all the ingredients are well incorporated.

9 Add the beef and broccoli and top with the sauce. Garnish with sesame seeds and enjoy!

Pro Tip

The vegetables are already cooked; you just want to take the frozen edge off of them.

MEATBALL & FRESH MOZZARELLA SUB

3 TO 4 SERVINGS | PREP: 20 MINUTES | COOK: 45 MINUTES

INGREDIENTS

1 pound ground beef

½ pound ground Italian sausage

2 eggs

¼ cup breadcrumbs

1 tablespoon minced garlic

1 tablespoon Worcestershire sauce

2 teaspoons garlic powder

2 teaspoons onion powder

1 teaspoon black pepper

1 teaspoon salt

½ teaspoon ground mustard

½ teaspoon red pepper flakes

Olive oil

1 batch Homemade Tomato Sauce (page 243)

3 to 4 hoagie rolls

6 to 8 fresh mozzarella slices

Chopped fresh basil (optional)

This is a perfect recipe to cater to a large crowd. And fresh mozzarella makes all the difference here! Feel free to make the meatballs as big or as little as you'd like. The meatballs could also be made ahead and frozen for a later date. There's plenty of flexibility in this easy but tasty dish.

1   In a large bowl, combine the beef, sausage, eggs, breadcrumbs, garlic, Worcestershire sauce, garlic powder, onion powder, black pepper, salt, mustard, and red pepper flakes.

2   Mix thoroughly, then form the mixture into 3- to 4-ounce balls (about the size of a clementine orange).

3   Heat a thin layer of olive oil in a large pan over medium heat. Add the meatballs and sear on both sides, 2 to 3 minutes per side. Set aside.

4   To the same pan, add a few cups of tomato sauce, then add your meatballs. Bring to a low simmer, cover, and allow the meatballs to finish cooking until tender and cooked through, another 15 to 20 minutes.

5   Preheat the oven to 400°F.

6   While the meatballs are cooking, slice the rolls, open them up, and toast them briefly (just enough so the bread won't get soggy) in the oven for 2 to 3 minutes.

7   Place the meatballs onto the bottom halves of the bread and add the mozzarella on top.

8   Place the meatball subs into the oven for about 5 minutes, until the cheese has melted and the bread is toasted. Garnish the inside of the sandwich with fresh basil, if using, and enjoy!

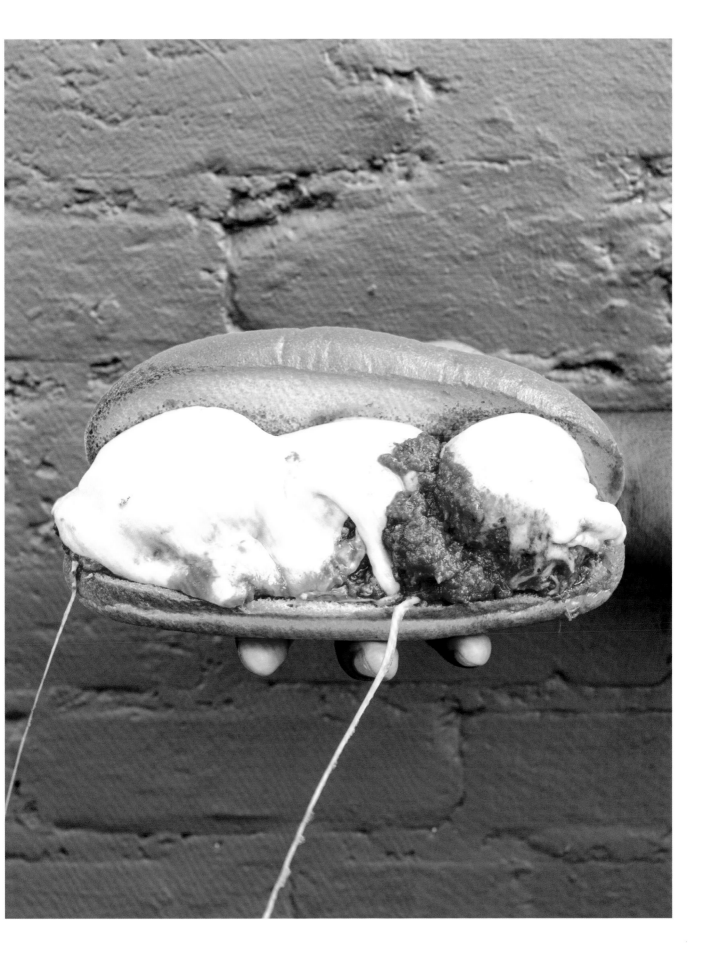

FRIED SALMON BLT

1 TO 2 SERVINGS	PREP: 10 MINUTES, PLUS 30 MINUTES TO MARINATE	COOK: 10 MINUTES

INGREDIENTS

1 cup buttermilk

½ cup hot sauce

Two 8-ounce pieces of salmon

5 strips thick-cut bacon

Neutral oil, for frying

2 brioche buns, halved

Sliced tomatoes

Romaine lettuce leaves

Flour Mixture

2 cups all-purpose flour

1 tablespoon garlic powder

1 tablespoon Old Bay seasoning

1 tablespoon onion powder

1 tablespoon black pepper

1 teaspoon cayenne

1 teaspoon lemon pepper

1 teaspoon salt (optional)

Sriracha Mayo

½ cup mayonnaise

1 tablespoon honey

1 tablespoon sriracha

A little backstory: One day, I was messing around in the kitchen and had the desire for a true BLT: lots of bacon, good bread, fresh tomatoes, and crisp lettuce. Well, me being me and wanting to try new things, I decided to fry up a piece of salmon. Listen…when I tell you this was one of my favorite things to eat for a solid month! Jazz it up with your favorite sauce and some fresh fries on the side.

1 In a small bowl, combine the buttermilk and hot sauce. Add the salmon, submerging the pieces completely. Cover with plastic wrap and place in the fridge for at least 30 minutes to marinate.

2 To a small pan over medium heat, add the bacon and cook until crispy, 4 to 5 minutes.

3 Preheat about 2½ cups of oil to 375°F in a medium pot.

4 **Make the flour mixture:** In a large bowl, mix the flour, garlic powder, Old Bay, onion powder, black pepper, cayenne, lemon pepper, and salt, if using.

5 Remove the salmon from the marinade, shaking off the excess buttermilk, and dip it into the flour. Coat the salmon thoroughly on all sides, then add it to the frying oil.

6 Fry until the salmon is extra crispy and floats to the top, 6 to 8 minutes (see Pro Tip).

7 **Make the sriracha mayo:** In a small bowl, mix the mayonnaise, honey, and sriracha.

8 Spread the mayo onto your brioche buns, then add the tomato, lettuce, bacon, and salmon.

9 Add more mayo on top of the salmon, if desired, and enjoy!

Pro Tip

Frying time may vary depending on the thickness of the salmon. If the salmon is floating at the top of the oil, it should be fully cooked.

JUMBO CRAB CAKE BLT
ON A CROISSANT

1 SERVING	PREP: 40 MINUTES	COOK: 35 MINUTES

INGREDIENTS

Crab Cake

8 ounces lump crab meat

1 small egg

Juice of 1 lemon

1 garlic clove, minced

1 teaspoon Worcestershire sauce

½ teaspoon black pepper

½ teaspoon Cajun seasoning

½ teaspoon chili powder

½ teaspoon garlic powder

½ teaspoon Old Bay seasoning

½ teaspoon onion powder

¼ cup panko breadcrumbs

2 teaspoons butter

Spicy Mayo

¼ cup mayonnaise

Juice of 1 lemon

½ teaspoon black pepper

½ teaspoon Cajun seasoning

½ teaspoon garlic powder

¼ teaspoon cayenne (optional)

1 large croissant, halved

2 teaspoons olive oil

3 strips thick-cut bacon, cooked

Sliced tomatoes

Romaine lettuce leaves

Crab cakes belong on a sandwich! The most important thing to keep in mind when making crab cakes is that less is more. You really want to be able to taste the crab and enjoy the texture of it. Everything else that goes into the crab cake should be minimal and complementary!

1 **Make the crab cake:** Lightly combine the crab meat, egg, lemon juice, garlic, Worcestershire sauce, black pepper, Cajun seasoning, chili powder, Old Bay, and onion powder in a medium bowl. Ensure the crab meat stays as whole as possible.

2 Sprinkle in the breadcrumbs and gently mix until the mixture is firm. Gently press the mixture into one large crab cake, then refrigerate for 10 to 15 minutes to firm up.

3 Preheat the oven to 350°F. Heat a large cast-iron skillet over medium heat, then add the butter and olive oil to coat the bottom of the pan.

4 Gently place the crab cake into the pan and allow to slowly brown from the bottom up for 4 to 5 minutes. Do not flip!

5 Transfer the skillet to the oven and cook for about 10 minutes, until the crab cake is lightly golden brown on top. Turn the oven to broil to brown the top of the crab cake for 60 seconds. Remove from the oven.

6 **Make the spicy mayo:** In a small bowl, mix the mayonnaise, lemon juice, black pepper, Cajun seasoning, garlic powder, and cayenne, if using.

7 Spread the spicy mayo on both halves of the croissant, then add the tomato, lettuce, and bacon. Carefully add the crab cake, then add the top half of the croissant. Enjoy!

CHEESY CHICKEN BIRRIA TACOS

| 12 TO 15 TACOS | PREP: 20 MINUTES | COOK: 90 MINUTES |

INGREDIENTS

2½ pounds chicken breast,
  cut into chunks

1 medium yellow onion, quartered

5 dried California chiles, seeded

5 garlic cloves

2 teaspoons garlic powder

2 teaspoons onion powder

2 teaspoons black pepper

1 teaspoon salt

1 teaspoon sazón

2 chicken bouillon cubes

4 bay leaves

1 pound Oaxaca cheese, shredded

10 to 12 street-style flour or
  corn tortillas

These can be called mini quesadillas, tacos, or quesatacos. Call them whatever you want—just make sure you have an appetite! Filled with savory juicy chicken, cheesy, and dipped in a delicious broth, these are guaranteed to be your new favorite taco!

1 To a large pot, add 8 cups of water. Add the chicken, onion, chiles, garlic, garlic powder, onion powder, black pepper, salt, sazón, bouillon, and bay leaves.

2 Bring to a boil, then reduce to a simmer for at least 30 minutes.

3 Transfer the onion, chiles, garlic, and ½ cup of the broth to a blender and blend to form a thick sauce. Return the mixture to the pot.

4 Simmer on low for another 30 minutes to 1 hour, until the chicken is falling apart. Transfer the chicken to a large bowl.

5 Shred the chicken with two forks, then slowly add some of the consomé broth into the bowl, until the chicken is saucy, not watery. Save the rest of the broth for dipping.

6 Heat a medium pan over medium heat. Dip a tortilla into the consomé, then transfer to the pan. Immediately cover the tortilla with cheese, then add the chicken to one side of the tortilla. Top with more cheese and cook until melted, 1 to 3 minutes.

7 Fold the tortilla over the filling and flip until the taco is golden brown on both sides, 1 to 2 minutes. Remove from the pan.

8 Repeat steps 6 and 7 with the remaining chicken, cheese, and tortillas. Dip in the consomé and enjoy!

CREAMY SPINACH-STUFFED SALMON

2 SERVINGS	PREP: 25 MINUTES	COOK: 15 MINUTES

INGREDIENTS

Salmon

One 8- to 10-ounce piece center-cut Alaskan salmon

½ teaspoon black pepper

½ teaspoon chili powder

½ teaspoon garlic powder

½ teaspoon lemon pepper

½ teaspoon Old Bay seasoning

½ teaspoon onion powder

2 tablespoons olive oil

Spinach Filling

6 ounces frozen chopped spinach, thawed

4 ounces cream cheese, softened

2 garlic cloves, minced

1 teaspoon black pepper

1 teaspoon garlic powder

1 teaspoon onion powder

½ teaspoon chili powder

¼ teaspoon lemon pepper

Broccoli

1 tablespoon unsalted butter

½ cup broccoli florets

½ teaspoon garlic powder

¼ teaspoon salt

¼ teaspoon black pepper

When a food is stuffed with another food, that's definitely a sign that it'll taste good. This stuffed salmon recipe is one of my favorites—it's delicious and very filling! Instead of going out to a fancy restaurant and paying an arm and a leg, try this recipe with a glass of wine. I promise you'll be cooking at home from now on when you have a craving for a fancy meal!

1   Preheat the oven to 375°F.

2   **Make the salmon:** Cut a slit into the side of the salmon to form a pocket, ensuring not to cut all the way through.

3   In a small bowl, mix the black pepper, chili powder, garlic powder, lemon pepper, Old Bay, and onion powder. Season all sides of the salmon, including inside the pocket.

4   **Make the spinach mixture:** In a medium bowl, combine the spinach, cream cheese, garlic, black pepper, garlic powder, onion powder, chili powder, and lemon pepper. Stuff the mixture into the salmon pocket.

5   Heat the oil in a medium pan over medium heat. Add the salmon, flesh side down. Cook for 3 to 5 minutes, then flip and cook until the skin begins to crisp, another 3 minutes. Transfer the pan to the oven and cook for 5 to 7 minutes, until the salmon reaches your desired temperature.

6   **Make the broccoli:** While the salmon is cooking, briefly heat another medium pan to medium heat. Add the butter, broccoli florets, garlic powder, salt, and black pepper. Cook until crisp-tender, 3 to 4 minutes. Enjoy!

JALAPEÑO CRAB & SHRIMP TACOS
WITH CHIPOTLE RANCH

12 TO 15 TACOS	PREP: 20 MINUTES	COOK: 30 MINUTES

INGREDIENTS

1 pound medium shrimp, peeled and deveined

2 teaspoons garlic powder

1½ teaspoons Old Bay seasoning

1 teaspoon black pepper

1 teaspoon onion powder

1 teaspoon sazón

1 to 3 tablespoons olive oil, divided

2 jalapeños, seeded and diced

8 ounces lump crab meat

1½ cups shredded cheddar

12 to 15 street-style flour tortillas

2 lemons, quartered (optional)

Chipotle Ranch

1 to 2 cups Easy Buttermilk Ranch (page 239)

2 tablespoons diced chipotle peppers in adobo sauce

This recipe is the perfect balance of spice, cheese, and seafood. Paired with a tasty chipotle ranch sauce, these tacos are sure to have you doubling up the recipe! There is just something about the pairing of crab and shrimp with jalapeño. Eat at your own risk— you may end up eating too many!

1   **Make the tacos:** In a large bowl, combine the shrimp, garlic powder, Old Bay, black pepper, onion powder, and sazón.

2   Heat 1 tablespoon of olive oil in a medium pan over medium heat and add the jalapeños. Cook until tender, 2 to 3 minutes.

3   Add the shrimp and cook until pink and cooked through, 3 to 4 minutes. Add the crab, then sprinkle in ¼ cup cheddar. Stir to combine, then remove from the heat and set aside.

4   In another medium pan, heat 1 teaspoon olive oil over medium heat. Place a tortilla in the pan. Add enough cheddar to lightly cover the tortilla, then add the crab and shrimp filling to half of the tortilla and cook until the cheese melts, 1 to 2 minutes. Fold the tortilla in half, then flip and cook for another minute to brown both sides.

5   Repeat with the remaining tortillas and filling, adding more oil for each set of tacos.

6   **Make the chipotle ranch:** In a small bowl, mix the ranch dressing and chipotles.

7   Serve the tacos with the ranch, garnish with fresh lemon wedges (if desired), and enjoy!

HONEY FRIED CHICKEN WINGS

12 CHICKEN WINGETTES | PREP: 20 MINUTES | COOK: 20 MINUTES

INGREDIENTS

12 chicken wingettes
3 eggs, beaten
½ cup milk
¼ cup hot sauce
1½ teaspoons sazón
1 teaspoon garlic powder
1 teaspoon onion powder
Neutral oil, for frying
¼ cup honey

Flour Mixture

2 cups all-purpose flour
1 tablespoon black pepper
1 tablespoon cayenne
1 tablespoon garlic powder
1 tablespoon Italian seasoning
1 tablespoon onion powder
1 tablespoon paprika
1½ teaspoons sazón

Simple. Classic. Delicious. Fried chicken is one of the finer things in life—full of flavor, texture, and good feelings in your stomach. Paired with almost anything, it will always be the star of the show. Spice up your flour mixture, drizzle the fried chicken with honey, and you will end up with the perfect bite every single time!

1   **Prepare the chicken:** In a large bowl, combine the chicken, eggs, milk, hot sauce, sazón, garlic powder, and onion powder (see Pro Tip 1).

2   **Make the flour mixture:** In a separate large bowl, mix the flour, black pepper, cayenne, garlic powder, Italian seasoning, onion powder, paprika, and sazón.

3   Fill a medium pot halfway with oil and heat to 375°F.

4   Toss the chicken wings in the flour mixture until completely covered, then let sit for 1 to 2 minutes.

5   Fry the wings, in batches if necessary, until golden brown and extra crispy, 10 to 12 minutes (see Pro Tip 2).

6   Transfer the wings to a wire rack. Immediately drizzle with honey.

Pro Tips

1   The chicken can sit in the marinade for 30 minutes to overnight for extra flavor!

2   Taste one of your wings after frying to determine if it's spicy enough. If not, add more cayenne to the flour mix.

DINNER

When you think of dinner, what do you think of? Is it comfort-style food, quick 30-minute one-pan dishes, or takeout on a Friday night? It doesn't matter what dinner is for you—there are no restrictions!

Breakfast for dinner was one of my favorite things growing up. My parents, my brothers, and I would all gather in the kitchen at night to make breakfast foods. There's something about eating pancakes at 8:30 at night that just makes them taste way better! Nowadays, I take the time to appreciate a break from reality, sit down, and enjoy a good dinner. Talk about your day, then get ready for bed or fall asleep watching your favorite TV show.

Two of my favorite recipes in the book are in this chapter: Hearty Beef Stew (page 140) and Classic Chicken Parmesan (page 139). I not only absolutely love these recipes, but they really embody what dinner is to me. The beef stew is hearty, cooked low and slow, and it fills the house with the most amazing smells! The chicken Parmesan is such a flavorful dish, perfect by itself, served with pasta, or eaten like a sandwich. No matter what your preference is, dinner can be good any kind of way.

HONEY-CHIPOTLE SALMON

3 TO 4 SERVINGS	PREP: 5 MINUTES	COOK: 5 MINUTES

INGREDIENTS

Three 8-ounce skinless salmon filets

1 teaspoon garlic powder

1 teaspoon onion powder

1 teaspoon chili powder

1 teaspoon black pepper

1 teaspoon Italian seasoning

½ teaspoon salt

2 tablespoons olive oil

½ cup honey

¼ cup lime juice

¼ cup orange juice

1½ tablespoons diced chipotle peppers in adobo sauce

Fresh lime zest (optional)

Can anyone tell me why salmon is just so good? You can make it a million different ways and it always comes out just right. Bears eat it straight out of the water, so we're not the only ones who have a true love for salmon! This delicious salmon recipe is the perfect addition to any weeknight meal. Pair it with Sweet Potato Mash (page 184) and you've got yourself a winner!

1   Season your salmon with garlic powder, onion powder, chili powder, black pepper, Italian seasoning, and salt.

2   Heat a pan to medium-high heat, then add the oil. Add the salmon and cook until nicely seared, 3 to 4 minutes per side. Set aside.

3   Reduce the heat to low and add the honey, lime juice, orange juice, and chipotles to the pan. Stir, scraping up the seasoning on the bottom of the pan, and allow the sauce to thicken slightly, 4 to 5 minutes.

4   Brush or pour the sauce onto the salmon filets, top with lime zest if desired, and enjoy!

LAMB CHOP & SALMON
SURF 'N' TURF PASTA

2 TO 3 SERVINGS	PREP: 15 MINUTES	COOK: 30 MINUTES

INGREDIENTS

Salt

1 pound fettuccine

1 batch Homemade Alfredo Sauce
(page 236)

1 tablespoon olive oil

½ pound medium asparagus spears,
trimmed

Salt

Black pepper

1 lemon, halved

Chopped fresh parsley

Salmon

1 teaspoon black pepper

1 teaspoon Cajun seasoning

1 teaspoon chili powder

1 teaspoon garlic powder

1 teaspoon lemon pepper

1 teaspoon Old Bay seasoning

1 teaspoon onion powder

Two 8-ounce pieces center-cut
Alaskan salmon, skin removed
(see Pro Tip 1)

1 tablespoon olive oil

1 thyme sprig

1 tablespoon unsalted butter

Lamb Chops

1 teaspoon black pepper

1 teaspoon chili powder

1 teaspoon garlic powder

1 teaspoon onion powder

1 teaspoon salt

8 lamb chops

1 tablespoon olive oil

1 thyme sprig

1 tablespoon unsalted butter

I'm fairly new to the lamb chop team. I only tried them for the first time about three years ago, and now they're one of my favorite proteins to eat! Lamb chops aren't as tough as steak, and they have a naturally sweet flavor. They're a perfect match for this pasta. Find somebody to enjoy this recipe with, as it's certainly enough for two!

1 Bring a large pot of salted water to a boil and cook the fettuccine until tender, 10 to 12 minutes. Drain and set aside.

2 Pour the Alfredo sauce into a small saucepan over low heat to keep warm.

3 **Prepare the salmon:** Mix the black pepper, Cajun seasoning, chili powder, garlic powder, lemon pepper, Old Bay, and onion powder in a small bowl. Season both sides of the salmon with the mixture.

4 **Prepare the lamb chops:** Mix the black pepper, chili powder, garlic powder, onion powder, and salt in a small bowl. Season both sides of the lamb chops with the mixture.

5 **Cook the salmon and lamb:** Heat two sauté pans over medium heat. Add 1 tablespoon of olive oil to each pan, then add a thyme sprig to each.

6 To one pan, add the salmon. Cook until nicely seared, 3 to 5 minutes. Add 1 tablespoon of butter, flip, and cook until the salmon is seared on the other side, about 5 minutes, basting with butter occasionally. Remove the salmon from the pan.

7 To the other pan, add the lamb chops, in batches if necessary, and cook until a nice crust forms, 2 to 3 minutes. Add 1 tablespoon of butter, flip, and cook until seared on the other side, 2 to 3 minutes, basting with butter occasionally (see Pro Tip 2). Remove the lamb chops from the pan.

8 Heat 1 tablespoon of olive oil in another medium pan over medium heat. Add the asparagus, lightly season with salt and pepper, add the juice from half of the lemon, and sauté until crisp-tender, 3 to 5 minutes.

9 Toss the pasta in the Alfredo sauce and divide among plates, layering the salmon and lamb chops on top with the asparagus on the side. Garnish with parsley and squeeze more lemon juice on top if desired.

Pro Tips

1 Remove the skin from the salmon by gently pulling the skin on the thicker side (where the skin is darker) away from the flesh.

2 The lamb chops may take longer to cook depending on their thickness. Thinner lamb chops will cook quickly and sear quickly. Thicker chops will sear quickly but will not cook through quickly. Aim for medium or medium-well for this recipe!

BAKED ZITI

6 TO 8 SERVINGS	PREP: 5 MINUTES	COOK: 35 MINUTES

INGREDIENTS

1 pound ziti

1 pound Italian sausage

1 pound ground turkey

2½ teaspoons garlic powder

2½ teaspoons onion powder

2½ teaspoons Italian seasoning

2½ teaspoons black pepper

1 teaspoon salt (optional)

2 tablespoons garlic paste

3 to 4 cups Homemade Tomato Sauce (page 243; see Pro Tip)

32 ounces ricotta

2 cups shredded mozzarella

Chopped fresh parsley

Don't bite my head off for this thought, but are lasagna and baked ziti pretty interchangeable? I know, I know, there's a true love and craftsmanship that goes into making a delicious lasagna. But when I was growing up, baked ziti was our go-to if we wanted a lasagna-style dinner with half of the work! Hope you enjoy this recipe, and don't forget the salad and garlic bread on the side!

1   Bring a medium pot of water to a boil. Add the pasta and cook until just al dente, 8 to 10 minutes. Drain and set aside.

2   Preheat the oven to 350°F.

3   To a large pot over medium heat, add the sausage and turkey. Cook until fully browned, about 10 minutes, breaking the meat into small pieces.

4   Pat the meat with a paper towel to remove some of the grease. Season with garlic powder, onion powder, Italian seasoning, black pepper, and salt, if using. Add the garlic paste, then stir in the tomato sauce, 1 cup at a time, until you reach your desired sauciness. Remove from the heat and let cool.

5   Add the ricotta and ziti. Mix thoroughly to coat.

6   Transfer to a baking dish, top with mozzarella, and bake for at least 20 minutes, until the crust is bubbly. Top with parsley and enjoy!

Pro Tip

Save some extra sauce to top the ziti after baking.

FRIED SHRIMP RAVIOLI

3 TO 4 SERVINGS	PREP: 50 MINUTES	COOK: 15 MINUTES

INGREDIENTS

Neutral oil, for frying

1 teaspoon olive oil

1 pound raw shrimp, diced

1 tablespoon garlic paste

½ teaspoon onion powder

½ teaspoon paprika

½ teaspoon black pepper

¼ teaspoon cayenne

4 ounces cream cheese, softened

½ cup grated Parmesan

½ cup frozen spinach,
  thawed and drained

Juice of ½ lemon

30 wonton wrappers

To Serve

Homemade Alfredo Sauce (page 236)

Homemade Tomato Sauce (page 243)

This is where we start to get creative…imagine a pizza roll, but made gourmet and filled with shrimp and spinach. It's amazing what you can come up with when you're trying to use up whatever you have left in your refrigerator! Make a bunch of these, throw them in the freezer, and save them for later.

1 To a small pan over medium heat, add the olive oil and shrimp. Cook until the shrimp is pink and fully cooked, 3 to 4 minutes, then transfer to a large bowl.

2 Add the garlic paste, onion powder, paprika, black pepper, and cayenne to the bowl and mix well.

3 Fold in the cream cheese, Parmesan, and spinach. Squeeze in the lemon juice and mix.

4 Drop a ½ tablespoon of filling onto a wonton wrapper.

5 Place another wonton wrapper on top. Using a small bowl of water, wet your fingers, then press the edges together. Fold all four edges up toward the center of the ravioli, crimping them closed with a fork.

6 Repeat steps 4 and 5 with the remaining wonton wrappers and filling.

7 Preheat about 1½ cups of frying oil to 375°F in a medium pot.

8 Add the ravioli, in batches if necessary, to the oil and fry until golden brown, 1 to 2 minutes.

9 Transfer to a paper towel-lined plate to drain. Enjoy!

TWICE-BAKED LOADED CHICKEN & BROCCOLI POTATOES

3 SERVINGS	PREP: 20 MINUTES	COOK: 80 MINUTES

INGREDIENTS

3 large russet potatoes

2 tablespoons olive oil , divided

1 pound chicken breast, cubed

1 small broccoli crown, chopped

1 teaspoon chili powder

1 teaspoon garlic powder

1 teaspoon dried oregano

1 teaspoon black pepper,
  plus more to taste

¼ cup sour cream

3 tablespoons butter, melted

Salt

1 cup shredded Colby Jack

Bacon bits (optional)

Whoever came up with the idea of twice-baked potatoes is a genius! Baked potatoes can be a simple but delicious side dish. Here, instead of eating the potato on the side, you stuff a whole meal into the potato, top it with cheese, and bake it to perfection.

1   Preheat the oven to 400°F. Lightly cover the potatoes with 1 tablespoon of oil then wrap in foil. Bake for about 1 hour, until tender.

2   Meanwhile, season your chicken with chili powder, garlic powder, oregano, and black pepper.

3   To a medium pan over medium heat, add 1 tablespoon of oil and your chicken. Cook until the chicken is cooked through, 7 to 8 minutes (see Pro Tip 1).

4   Remove the chicken from the pan and add the broccoli. Add ½ cup water and allow the broccoli to cook until slightly tender, 4 to 5 minutes (see Pro Tip 2).

5   Remove the potatoes from the foil, cut them lengthwise down the middle, making sure not to cut all the way through. Gently press to open the potato halves. Scoop out about half of the potato flesh and transfer to a bowl.

6   Add the sour cream and butter to the bowl. Season lightly with salt and pepper, mix, then add back to the potato shells.

7   Add the chicken and broccoli, then top with cheese.

8   Place the potatoes back into the oven and bake for 5 to 10 minutes, until the cheese is melted and beginning to brown.

9   Top with bacon bits if desired and enjoy!

Pro Tips

1   If you're not sure if the chicken is done, treat yourself by breaking a cube open and tasting it. (Make sure the chicken is no longer pink on the inside!)

2   For softer broccoli, throw it in a microwave-safe bowl and steam until tender, 5 to 8 minutes.

GREAT-GRANDMA'S CHICKEN & DUMPLINGS

4 TO 5 SERVINGS	PREP: 25 MINUTES	COOK: 2 HOURS

INGREDIENTS

1 whole chicken

2 celery stalks, chopped

1 small onion, cut into wedges

3 cups chicken broth

3 teaspoons garlic powder

3 teaspoons onion powder

3 teaspoons Italian seasoning

3 teaspoons black pepper

1 teaspoon smoked paprika

1½ to 2 teaspoons salt

Dumplings

2 cups all-purpose flour, plus more for dusting

2 teaspoons garlic powder

4 tablespoons butter, softened

½ to ¾ cup chicken broth

Shoutout to my late great-grandmother—this dish truly reminds me of her, and I can almost taste it as I'm writing this! Chicken and dumplings is a meal that will have you warm on the inside, wrapped up in a blanket on any given day.

1   To a large pot, add the chicken, celery, onion, chicken broth, and 3 cups water. Bring to a boil and skim off any impurities (the white and gray stuff that floats to the top).

2   Add the garlic powder, onion powder, Italian seasoning, black pepper, paprika, and salt. Continue boiling for 1½ to 2 hours, until the meat begins to fall off the bone.

3   Remove from the heat and let cool. Shred the chicken, set aside with the vegetables, and discard the bones.

4   **Make the dumplings:** In a large bowl, combine the flour, garlic powder, and butter. Mix thoroughly, then add the broth, ¼ cup at a time, mixing until you get a workable dough.

5   On a floured surface, roll out the dough to about ½-inch thick and slice into small rectangles.

6   Bring the broth back to a boil, then add in your dumplings one at a time (see Pro Tip). Reduce to a low boil and cook for 15 to 20 minutes.

7   Add the chicken and vegetables back in, reduce to a low simmer, and cook for another 10 minutes, until the dumplings are tender and everything in the pot has come together. Adjust the seasonings to taste. Enjoy!

Pro Tip

Don't add the dumplings all at once or they'll stick to each other.

TURKEY MEATLOAF

4 TO 5 SERVINGS	PREP: 15 MINUTES	COOK: 45 MINUTES

INGREDIENTS

1½ pounds ground turkey

½ cup mild salsa

1 cup italian breadcrumbs

1 large egg

1 tablespoon Worcestershire sauce

1½ teaspoons garlic powder

1½ teaspoons onion powder

1½ teaspoons Italian seasoning

1½ teaspoons black pepper

½ teaspoon salt

½ cup ketchup

¼ cup honey

1½ tablespoons apple cider vinegar

Meatloaf is one of those meals: You either hate it or love it. For some reason, some people look at meatloaf as something they don't want on their plate, but let me tell you something: This meatloaf is going to be the star of the show! The best part about it is it's so easy to make.

1 Preheat the oven to 375°F.

2 In a large bowl, combine the turkey, salsa, breadcrumbs, egg, Worcestershire sauce, garlic powder, onion powder, Italian seasoning, black pepper, and salt. Mix thoroughly.

3 Transfer the mixture to a baking dish or loaf pan, then form it into a loaf. Bake for 40 to 45 minutes, until the meatloaf is cooked through and the juices run clear when cut.

4 In a small bowl, mix the ketchup, honey, and vinegar. Spread the mixture onto the meatloaf.

5 Place the pan back into the oven for another 5 to 10 minutes, until the glaze is caramelized.

6 Let rest for 5 minutes, then slice and enjoy!

CLASSIC CHICKEN PARMESAN

4 TO 5 SERVINGS	PREP: 30 MINUTES	COOK: 40 MINUTES

INGREDIENTS

2 pounds chicken breast

2 teaspoons black pepper, divided

2 teaspoons garlic powder, divided

2 teaspoons onion powder, divided

2 teaspoons smoked paprika, divided

3 large eggs

1 teaspoon Old Bay seasoning

1 cup all-purpose flour

2 cups Italian breadcrumbs

¼ cup grated Parmesan

Neutral oil, for frying

2 cups Homemade Tomato Sauce (page 243)

1 to 2 cups shredded mozzarella

Chopped fresh parsley

I get asked all the time: *Zo, what's your favorite food?* I almost always never have an answer. But if I had to name my top ten, chicken Parmesan is definitely in there! It reminds me of fun times growing up, as this recipe is one of my father's specialties.

1   Preheat the oven to 350°F.

2   Cut the chicken into four even pieces. Gently flatten the chicken out with a meat tenderizer to ½-inch thick. In a small bowl mix together and season the chicken with 1 teaspoon each of black pepper, garlic powder, onion powder, and paprika.

3   In a shallow bowl, combine the eggs and Old Bay. Mix well.

4   In a separate shallow bowl, combine the flour and the remaining 1 teaspoon each of black pepper, garlic powder, onion powder, and paprika. Mix well.

5   In a shallow bowl, mix the breadcrumbs and Parmesan. Working with one piece at a time, coat both sides of the chicken in the flour, then with the egg mixture, and finally with the breadcrumbs. Set aside.

6   Add about 1 inch of oil to a large frying pan over medium heat. Fry the chicken, in batches if necessary, until golden brown, 2 minutes on each side. Place the chicken briefly onto a paper towel or wire rack to drain.

7   To a baking dish, add half of the marinara sauce. Add the chicken, followed by the remaining marinara. Top with mozzarella.

8   Bake for 15 to 20 minutes, until the cheese is nice and bubbly. Top with fresh parsley and enjoy!

HEARTY BEEF STEW

| 5 SERVINGS | PREP: 25 MINUTES | COOK: 3 HOURS |

INGREDIENTS

2 pounds beef chuck roast, cubed

2 teaspoons garlic powder

2 teaspoons onion powder

2 teaspoons black pepper

1½ teaspoons salt

2 tablespoons olive oil

1 medium yellow onion, diced

3 celery stalks, diced

3 carrots, chopped

5 garlic cloves, minced

2 tablespoons tomato paste

3 to 4 cups chicken broth, divided

3 to 4 cups beef broth, divided

4 medium russet potatoes, cubed

3 bay leaves

2 thyme sprigs

3 tablespoons cornstarch

Cooked rice (optional)

There's nothing like a big pot of beef stew cooking on the stove all day, filling the entire house with the most amazing smells! Is it me or do the dishes that take the longest to cook always taste the best? Waiting hours and hours to taste the final product is so rewarding!

1   In a large bowl, season the beef with garlic powder, onion powder, black pepper, and salt.

2   Heat the oil in a large pot over high heat and add the beef. Cook until all the sides are seared, 3 to 4 minutes total, then remove from the pan.

3   Reduce the heat to medium and add your onion, celery, carrots, and garlic. Cook until the vegetables are fragrant, 4 to 5 minutes, gently scraping the bottom of the pan.

4   Add the tomato paste and mix well to coat, then deglaze the pan with about 1 cup of chicken broth. Gently scrape the bottoms and sides of the pan to ensure no flavor is left behind!

5   Return your beef to the pot, followed by 2 cups each of chicken broth and beef broth, the bay leaves, and thyme.

6   Cover the pot and let simmer for about 90 minutes, stirring occasionally (see Pro Tip).

7   Add your potatoes, cover the pot, and simmer for another 90 minutes, until the meat is tender and the vegetables are soft. Remove the bay leaves and thyme and discard.

8   In a small bowl, mix the cornstarch and 5 tablespoons of water to make a slurry, then add to the pot and stir until the broth thickens into a light gravy, 2 minutes.

9   Serve over rice or eat by itself. Enjoy!

Pro Tip

If your broth reduces too much while simmering, add more chicken or beef broth, ½ cup at a time, until it reaches your desired consistency.

GLAZED BBQ PORK CHOPS

2 TO 3 SERVINGS	PREP: 5 MINUTES, PLUS 30 MINUTES TO MARINATE	COOK: 15 MINUTES

INGREDIENTS

1 pound bone-in thick-cut pork chops (2 to 3 chops)

½ cup pineapple juice

1 to 2 teaspoons brown sugar

1 teaspoon chili powder

1 teaspoon garlic powder

1 teaspoon onion powder

1 teaspoon black pepper

1 teaspoon salt

1 cup BBQ sauce

½ cup orange juice

One night when I was a young kid, my grandfather, Pop Pop, was making the most delicious pork chops. Me being me, I was intent on making a pork chop sandwich and taking it to school for lunch the next day. But my mother told me I couldn't, because it was a bone-in pork chop. After a long back and forth, I ended up taking it anyway and just eating around the bone. Moral of the story: Don't let anything stop you from enjoying what you want to eat!

1   Fire up your grill (or flat-top griddle) and allow the charcoal to get hot (350 to 400°F), about 30 minutes. Make one side of the grill your hot zone and the other side a cool zone.

2   To a zipper bag, add your pork chops, pineapple juice, brown sugar, chili powder, garlic powder, onion powder, black pepper, and salt. Rub the marinade all over the pork chops and allow them to marinate in the refrigerator for 30 minutes to 1 hour (see Pro Tip 1).

3   In a small bowl, mix the barbecue sauce and orange juice to make a glaze.

4   Place the pork chops on the hot side of the grill. Cook for about 5 minutes, then flip. Cook until a nice crust has formed on both sides, another 5 minutes.

5   Brush a light layer of glaze onto the pork chop, then flip and glaze the other side. Move the pork chops to the cool side of the grill and close the lid (see Pro Tip 2).

6   After a few minutes, open the lid, glaze the pork chops again, and close the lid. Repeat this process one more time, flipping the pork chop, until the pork chop is fully glazed and the glaze is caramelized.

7   Remove from the grill and enjoy!

Pro Tips

1   Don't marinate for too long, as the pineapple juice will begin to break down the pork chop.

2   This will help the sauce stick to the pork chop.

CHEESY CHICKEN FAJITAS

2 TO 3 SERVINGS	PREP: 10 MINUTES	COOK: 10 MINUTES

INGREDIENTS

1 pound chicken breast, sliced into thin strips

1 teaspoon chili powder

1 teaspoon garlic powder

1 teaspoon smoked paprika

½ teaspoon ground cumin

½ teaspoon black pepper

½ teaspoon salt

1 to 2 teaspoons olive oil

⅓ green bell pepper, sliced

⅓ red bell pepper, sliced

¼ red onion, sliced

½ cup shredded Colby Jack

Corn or flour tortillas, warmed (optional)

Imagine you're at a restaurant and you hear a sizzling skillet coming from around the corner and smell delicious fajitas in the air. All of a sudden, you know what you're going to order. That's the inspiration behind this dish, and remember to make it in a cast iron skillet—it'll taste better!

1 In a large bowl, combine the chicken, chili powder, garlic powder, paprika, cumin, black pepper, and salt.

2 Heat the oil in a medium pan over medium heat. Add your chicken and cook until you get a nice sear, 3 to 4 minutes.

3 Add the bell peppers and onion and cook until tender, 4 to 5 minutes.

4 Add ¼ cup water and scrape up the seasoning from the bottom of the pan. Give everything one final mix.

5 Top the pan with cheese, cover, and allow to melt for 2 to 3 minutes.

6 Serve with warm tortillas or by itself. Enjoy!

PEACH-GLAZED BAKED CHICKEN LEGS

5 TO 6 SERVINGS	PREP: 5 MINUTES, PLUS 1 HOUR TO MARINATE	COOK: 65 MINUTES

INGREDIENTS

1½ pounds chicken legs
1 cup olive oil
¼ cup brown sugar
1½ teaspoons chili powder
1½ teaspoons garlic powder
1½ teaspoons dried oregano
1½ teaspoons smoked paprika
1 teaspoon ground cumin
1 teaspoon salt

Peach Glaze

½ cup peach preserves
¼ cup honey
¼ cup ketchup
¼ cup Worcestershire sauce
2 tablespoons apple cider vinegar
1½ teaspoons chili powder

Think flavors of the summertime, but in December. In my opinion, there's nothing like a hot piece of barbecue-glazed chicken fresh off the grill. This recipe will replicate that perfectly for you, straight out of the oven! Pair it with a couple of your favorite sides and an ice-cold drink.

1 In a large bowl, combine the chicken, oil, brown sugar, chili powder, garlic powder, oregano, paprika, cumin, and salt. Mix well, cover, and allow to marinate in the refrigerator for 30 minutes to 1 hour.

2 Preheat the oven to 350°F. Place a wire rack on top of a baking sheet.

3 Transfer the chicken to the wire rack and bake for 30 to 45 minutes. Flip, then bake for about 30 minutes more, until browned and fully cooked.

4 **Make the glaze:** To a small pot over low heat, add the peach preserves, honey, ketchup, Worcestershire sauce, vinegar, and chili powder. Mix well.

5 Bring to a low simmer to fully incorporate, then remove from the heat and let cool.

6 Brush the glaze onto the chicken, increase the oven temperature to 400°F, and cook the chicken for another 5 to 10 minutes, until the glaze is sticky and caramelized.

7 Remove from the oven and enjoy!

SMOTHERED PORK CHOPS

4 TO 5 SERVINGS	PREP: 10 MINUTES	COOK: 45 MINUTES

INGREDIENTS

Neutral oil, for frying
2 pounds boneless pork chops
1 teaspoon olive oil
1 teaspoon garlic powder
1 teaspoon onion powder
1 teaspoon dried oregano
1 teaspoon smoked paprika
1 teaspoon black pepper
½ teaspoon salt
1 cup all-purpose flour
Cooked rice or potatoes, for serving

Gravy

½ small onion, sliced
2 tablespoons all-purpose flour
1½ cups beef broth
Salt
Black pepper

What is it about anything "smothered" and served over rice that tastes so good? Maybe it's the tender meat, the full-stomach feeling, or the warmth and comfort you have while eating it. Whatever it is for you, these smothered pork chops will have you running back for seconds and thirds!

1   In a large pan, heat ½ to 1 inch of frying oil over medium heat.

2   Season the pork chops with olive oil, garlic powder, onion powder, oregano, paprika, black pepper, and salt (see Pro Tip 1).

3   Place the flour in a shallow bowl, then dip the pork chops into the flour and transfer directly into the hot oil. Fry until almost cooked through, about 3 minutes per side, then remove them from the pan (see Pro Tip 2).

4   **Make the gravy:** Remove enough of the oil from the pan so only a thin layer remains, then add the onions. Cook over medium heat until they begin to change color, 2 to 3 minutes. Stir in the flour, 1 tablespoon at a time, to form a roux.

5   Add the beef broth, stirring constantly, to form a thin gravy (see Pro Tip 3). Season with salt and pepper.

6   Return the pork chops to the pan, cover, and simmer over low heat for about 15 minutes to allow the pork chops to absorb some of the gravy, continue cooking, and tenderize.

7   Serve over rice or potatoes. Enjoy!

Pro Tips

1 The olive oil will help the seasonings stick to the meat.

2 Depending on the thickness of your pork chops, the cooking time may vary.

3 If the gravy is too thin, add more flour. If it's too thick, add more beef broth.

SPICY SAUSAGE & RICOTTA RIGATONI

5 TO 6 SERVINGS	PREP: 15 MINUTES	COOK: 20 MINUTES

INGREDIENTS

Salt

1 pound rigatoni

1 pound ground spicy Italian sausage

½ pound ground beef or turkey

1 teaspoon garlic powder

1 teaspoon Italian seasoning

1 teaspoon onion powder

1 teaspoon black pepper

1 teaspoon red pepper flakes (optional)

1½ to 2 cups Homemade Tomato Sauce (page 243)

1½ to 2 cups Homemade Alfredo Sauce (page 236)

1 cup ricotta

½ cup grated Parmesan

6 basil leaves, sliced

Rigatoni might be the best pasta shape out there. It holds the sauce perfectly, is the perfect size, and just reigns supreme in my book. I know many people have their opinions on ricotta—maybe they've had it one time and didn't like it—but listen, just give it a try. As I always say, I'll try anything twice!

1   Bring a medium pot of water to a boil, then add a pinch of salt and the rigatoni. Cook until tender, 8 to 10 minutes, then drain and set aside.

2   To a large pan over medium heat, add the sausage and ground beef. Cook, breaking up the meat with a spoon, until fully cooked, 8 to 10 minutes. Use a paper towel to remove almost all of the grease in the pan.

3   Season the meat with garlic powder, Italian seasoning, onion powder, black pepper, and red pepper flakes if using.

4   Add the tomato sauce and Alfredo sauce to the pan (see Pro Tip). Add your pasta and mix everything thoroughly.

5   In a small bowl, mix the ricotta and Parmesan. Drop spoonfuls of the mixture over the top of the pasta. (Do not mix in.)

6   Add the fresh basil and enjoy!

Pro Tip

Start with 1½ cups of each sauce, then add in your pasta. If you like a saucier dish, use 2 cups of each sauce.

CREAMY TUSCAN CHICKEN THIGHS

4 TO 5 SERVINGS	PREP: 20 MINUTES	COOK: 40 MINUTES

INGREDIENTS

2½ tablespoons butter, sliced

2 rosemary sprigs

2 thyme sprigs

1 pound bone-in chicken thighs

1 teaspoon garlic powder

1 teaspoon onion powder

1 teaspoon black pepper

½ teaspoon chili powder

½ teaspoon salt

1 tablespoon olive oil

Sauce

2 tablespoons butter

1 small shallot, diced

10 to 12 cherry tomatoes, halved

20 baby spinach leaves (about 1 cup)

1½ tablespoons sun-dried tomatoes, diced

5 garlic cloves, minced

1 to 1½ cups heavy cream

½ teaspoon red pepper flakes

¼ cup grated Parmesan

Salt

Black pepper

Simple, quick, and delicious. You have to use bone-in thighs for this, because that's where ALL the flavor is. The funny thing about chicken thighs is that many people don't realize they are the most flavorful part of the chicken and, arguably, the most versatile. Graduate from chicken breast and step into the world of thighs!

1   Preheat the oven to 375°F. Cover the bottom of a baking dish with the butter, then add the rosemary and thyme.

2   Season the chicken with garlic powder, onion powder, black pepper, chili powder, and salt.

3   Heat the oil in a large pan over medium-high heat. Add your chicken thighs, skin side down, and sear until a nice crust forms, about 3 minutes on each side.

4   Transfer to the baking dish, cover with foil, and bake for 25 to 30 minutes, until the thighs are fully cooked.

5   Remove the foil and increase the oven temperature to 400°F. Cook for another 5 minutes, until the chicken has a nice crispy crust.

6   **Make the sauce:** To the same large pan over medium heat, add the butter and shallot. Scrape up the bits at the bottom of the pan. Cook until fragrant, 2 to 3 minutes.

7   Add your cherry tomatoes, spinach, sun-dried tomatoes, and garlic (see Pro Tip), followed by 1 cup of heavy cream and the red pepper flakes. Bring to a low simmer, 4 to 5 minutes. Add the Parmesan, stir, and taste. Season lightly with salt and pepper, then simmer until creamy and thickened slightly, about 3 more minutes (see Pro Tip 2).

8   Transfer the chicken to the pan and cover with the sauce. Reduce the heat to low and allow the chicken to sit in the sauce for 3 to 4 minutes. Turn off the heat and enjoy!

Pro Tips

1   It's important to not add your garlic at the same time as the shallots, since garlic burns easily.

2   If the sauce is too thick, add more heavy cream, 1 tablespoon at a time. This can alter the flavor, so taste and adjust the seasoning if needed.

BEEF BIRRIA TACOS

ABOUT 20 TACOS | PREP: 1 HOUR | COOK: 4 HOURS

INGREDIENTS

5 pounds beef chuck roast, cut into large chunks

1 large onion, quartered

10 dried California chiles

5 garlic cloves

4 bay leaves

3 tablespoons chicken bouillon

1 tablespoon black pepper

1 tablespoon garlic powder

1 teaspoon onion powder

1 tablespoon salt

1 tablespoon sazón

Olive oil

20 street-style flour tortillas

1 pound shredded mozzarella

1 small onion, diced

1 bunch cilantro, chopped

If there were a picture of the perfect taco in the dictionary, you just might see these! Slow cooked for hours, cheesy, and dipped in their own consomé—my mouth is watering just thinking about them. If you have leftover beef, use it in any recipe you can think of—it is that good!

1   To a large pot add 5 quarts water, the chuck roast, and onion. Bring to a boil.

2   Use a spoon to skim off any impurities that come to the surface. Reduce the heat to medium, then add the chiles, garlic, bay leaves, chicken bouillon, black pepper, garlic powder, onion powder, salt, and sazón. Bring to a simmer until the liquid has reduced and the chuck roast is tender, about 3 hours.

3   Halfway through cooking, transfer the chiles, onion, garlic, and about ½ cup of the broth to a blender. Blend until smooth, then return the mixture to the pot. Continue to simmer.

4   Taste the consomé broth and add additional seasoning if needed. Remove the meat and shred with a fork, then add about ¼ cup of the broth to the meat.

5   Heat 1 teaspoon olive oil in a skillet over medium-low heat. Dip a tortilla into the consomé, then immediately transfer to the skillet. Sprinkle the tortilla with mozzarella, then add about 1½ tablespoons of beef and another layer of mozzarella. Repeat this process, adding more oil with every new tortilla.

6   When the cheese begins to melt, after about 2 minutes, fold the tortilla over the filling, then flip and cook for another 1 to 2 minutes to get the other side crispy.

7   Pour the consomé into a cup or bowl, then add the chopped onions and cilantro. Dip the tacos into the consomé and enjoy!

Pro Tip

If you have leftover meat, save it! You can use the leftovers in a variety of dishes, like pasta, ramen, or nachos.

SWEET & SOUR CHICKEN FRIED RICE

4 SERVINGS	PREP: 10 MINUTES	COOK: 30 MINUTES

INGREDIENTS

Sweet & Sour Sauce

¼ cup ketchup

¼ cup pineapple juice

¼ cup soy sauce

¼ cup sugar

¼ cup white vinegar

¼ teaspoon red pepper flakes

1 tablespoon cornstarch

Chicken

1 pound chicken breast, chopped

1 teaspoon garlic powder

1 teaspoon onion powder

1 teaspoon white pepper

¼ teaspoon salt

1½ teaspoons vegetable oil

Fried Rice

1 tablespoon butter

¼ cup diced onion

3 garlic cloves, minced

¼ cup frozen mixed vegetables

1 to 2 large eggs

3 cups cooked, day-old white rice

3 tablespoons soy sauce

1 teaspoon sesame oil

Sliced green onions

This is another one of my favorite takeout dishes that I found was so easy to make at home. The key here is to cook the chicken just until it's done, resulting in tender, perfectly cooked meat that's coated in the most delicious sweet and sour glaze. To switch the dish up, try substituting lo mein noodles instead of fried rice!

1 **Make the sauce:** To a small saucepan over medium heat, add the ketchup, pineapple juice, soy sauce, sugar, vinegar, and red pepper flakes. Mix and bring to a low simmer.

2 In a small bowl, mix the cornstarch and 3 tablespoons of water to make a slurry. Add the slurry to the pot and cook until thickened, 2 to 3 minutes, stirring occasionally.

3 **Make the chicken:** Season the chicken with garlic powder, onion powder, white pepper, and salt. To a large wok, add the vegetable oil, and turn the heat to medium-high. Add the chicken and cook until golden brown, 5 to 7 minutes. Remove from the pan and set aside.

4 **Make the fried rice:** Reduce the heat to medium. Add the butter, onion, and garlic. Cook until fragrant, 2 to 3 minutes, then add in your frozen veggies and eggs and cook until the eggs are scrambled and the vegetables are warmed through, 2 to 3 minutes.

5 Add your rice, soy sauce, and sesame oil. Mix until everything is a light brown color, 2 to 3 minutes.

6 Mix together the chicken and sauce. Divide the rice among bowls, then top with the chicken and garnish with green onions.

CRISPY CHICKEN PASTA

3 TO 4 SERVINGS	PREP: 20 MINUTES	COOK: 25 MINUTES

INGREDIENTS

Salt

1 pound penne

2 teaspoons garlic powder

2 teaspoons onion powder

2 teaspoons Italian seasoning

2 teaspoons smoked paprika

2 teaspoons black pepper

1½ pounds chicken breasts, pounded thin

1 cup all-purpose flour

2 cups panko breadcrumbs

3 eggs

Neutral oil, for frying

1 batch Homemade Alfredo Sauce (page 236)

25 baby spinach leaves (about 1 cup)

Chopped fresh parsley

Grated Parmesan

Crispy chicken and saucy pasta don't normally go together, but when I tell y'all this one is going to change the game, trust me! It has the perfect balance of texture from the crispy fried chicken and the creamy tender pasta. Throw in a few spinach leaves to make it healthy (the vegetables will make you strong!), and it just might beat a traditional chicken Alfredo.

1 Bring a medium pot of water to a boil. Add a pinch of salt and cook your penne until al dente, 8 to 12 minutes. Drain and set aside.

2 In a small bowl, combine the garlic powder, onion powder, Italian seasoning, paprika, black pepper, and 1½ teaspoons salt. Use half of this seasoning mix to season your chicken breast generously.

3 Place the flour and breadcrumbs each in a small bowl. Split the other half of the seasoning between the flour and the breadcrumbs. Whisk the eggs in a third bowl.

4 Fill a large pan with about 2 inches of oil and set over medium-high heat. Dip your chicken into the flour, then into the egg, and then finally into the breadcrumbs. Repeat until all the chicken is covered.

5 Fry each chicken breast until golden brown, flipping halfway through, 5 to 7 minutes.

6 To another large pan over low heat, add the Alfredo sauce and spinach, then add the pasta.

7 Slice the chicken and top the pasta. Garnish with fresh parsley and Parmesan and enjoy!

SALMON & CRAB PASTA

2 TO 3 SERVINGS	PREP: 5 MINUTES	COOK: 20 MINUTES

INGREDIENTS

Salt

1 pound fettuccine

Two 8-ounce salmon filets, cubed

½ teaspoon chili powder

½ teaspoon garlic powder

½ teaspoon dried oregano

½ teaspoon black pepper

½ teaspoon smoked paprika

1 tablespoon olive oil

1 tablespoon butter

1 batch Homemade Alfredo Sauce (page 236)

8 ounces lump crab meat

Chopped fresh parsley (optional)

Smoked paprika

Seafood and pasta are the perfect match! There's a popular opinion that seafood and cheese don't belong together, but I'm here to debunk that. Now that doesn't mean you should go pour nacho cheese on top of a piece of fish, but a little Parmesan in your sauce to coat this pasta is going to be amazing. Perfectly cooked seafood and a hearty amount of pasta is *chef's kiss!*

1   Bring a medium pot of water to a boil. Add a pinch of salt and the pasta. Cook until tender, 8 to 10 minutes. Drain and set aside.

2   Season your salmon with chili powder, garlic powder, oregano, pepper, paprika, and ¼ teaspoon salt.

3   Heat a medium pan over medium-high heat and add the oil. Once the pan is hot, add the salmon, flesh side down, and cook until you begin to see the salmon fold up slightly, 3 to 4 minutes. Flip and cook on the other side until fully cooked, 3 to 4 minutes.

4   Add the butter and baste the salmon for 1 to 2 minutes. Remove from the heat.

5   In a large bowl, toss your pasta in the Alfredo sauce and top with the salmon and crab pieces. Garnish with parsley, if desired, and paprika. Enjoy!

SIDES

What's a good meal without some amazing sides? In my experience, side dishes are either the whole meal or the best part of the meal! On Thanksgiving, you'll have some turkey of course, but it's the side dishes that you remember: Aunty's special this, Uncle's famous that, and you always have to have Grandma's signature Five-Cheese Mac & Cheese (page 168)!

There's no limit on what can be a side dish. I'm a firm believer that you should eat what you want, with whatever you want. If you want to have lasagna with a side of chicken Alfredo pasta, or a steak dinner with a side of sushi, that's perfectly fine!

Your sides can be whatever you want them to be; sometimes the awkward food combinations are just meant to be together. Spicy Dirty Rice (page 167) and Salmon Croquettes (page 55)? Air-Fried Blackened Chicken Tenders (page 73) and Homemade Alfredo Sauce (page 236)? Coquito (page 221) with a side of Grandma's Oatmeal Raisin Cookies (page 200)? Live life on the edge, create your own side dishes to pair with your meal, and enjoy the food however you like!

CHEESY SCALLOPED POTATOES

4 TO 5 SERVINGS	PREP: 50 MINUTES	COOK: 1 HOUR

INGREDIENTS

5 medium Yukon Gold potatoes

1 tablespoon unsalted butter

¼ small yellow onion, diced

3 garlic cloves, minced

1 tablespoon all-purpose flour

1 to 1½ cups heavy cream

1 teaspoon garlic powder

1 teaspoon dried oregano

1 teaspoon black pepper

1 teaspoon salt

½ teaspoon smoked paprika

4 ounces cream cheese, softened

¼ cup grated Romano cheese

½ cup shredded Colby Jack

Chopped fresh parsley

This side is a childhood staple of mine: thinly sliced potatoes layered on top of each other, baked with a creamy, cheesy sauce until bubbly and delicious! Growing up, I remember eating lots of dinners with a side of these potatoes, some type of vegetable, and a savory protein. Sometimes the simplest meals will forever hold a place in your heart.

1   Preheat the oven to 375°F. Peel and thinly slice the potatoes.

2   Heat the butter in a medium pot over medium heat, then add the onion and garlic. Cook until fragrant and translucent, 2 to 3 minutes.

3   Add the flour, then slowly stir in 1 cup of heavy cream (see Pro Tip) and mix thoroughly to incorporate the flour. The sauce should be thick but smooth.

4   Add the garlic powder, oregano, black pepper, salt, and paprika. Mix well and bring to a simmer.

5   Reduce the heat to low, then whisk in the cream cheese and Romano. Remove from the heat.

6   Layer an 8-inch square baking dish with potatoes and cheese sauce. Repeat with the remaining ingredients, finishing with a layer of cheese sauce.

7   Top with Colby Jack, cover with foil, and bake for 55 to 60 minutes, until the potatoes are tender. Uncover and bake for 10 more minutes, until golden brown and bubbly.

8   Let sit for about 10 to 15 minutes before serving. Garnish with parsley and enjoy!

Pro Tip

If your cheese sauce is too thick, add in the extra ½ cup of heavy cream.

SPICY DIRTY RICE

6 TO 8 SERVINGS | PREP: 10 MINUTES | COOK: 35 MINUTES

INGREDIENTS

2 cups white rice

4 cups chicken broth

½ small green bell pepper, diced

1 tablespoon butter

½ small red bell pepper, diced

½ small onion, diced

4 garlic cloves, minced

1 pound ground pork sausage

1 pound ground turkey

2 teaspoons black pepper

2 teaspoons garlic powder

2 teaspoons smoked paprika

1 teaspoon rubbed sage

1 teaspoon salt (optional)

½ to 1 teaspoon cayenne (optional)

Now, it's debatable whether this rice is actually a side dish. Because, quite frankly, it can easily be a main. It's full of flavor, has the perfect amount of spice, and is so filling! One of the things I love about this dish is that it's very customizable—anything you throw in the pot will taste good. Season it up and you can't go wrong!

1 In a large pot, bring the rice and broth to a boil. Reduce to a simmer and cook until the rice is tender and the liquid has absorbed, about 20 minutes, then remove from the heat. Fluff with a fork and set aside.

2 To a large pan, add the butter, bell pepper, and onion. Cook over medium heat until softened, 3 to 4 minutes, then add the garlic (see Pro Tip).

3 Add the sausage and turkey and cook, breaking up the meat with a spatula, until browned and fully cooked through, about 10 minutes.

4 Stir in the black pepper, garlic powder, paprika, sage, and salt and cayenne, if using. Add the rice and mix well. Taste and adjust the seasoning. Enjoy!

Pro Tip

For saucier rice, add a few teaspoons of flour and chicken broth when cooking the vegetables to create a gravy.

FIVE-CHEESE MAC & CHEESE

8 TO 10 SERVINGS	PREP: 25 MINUTES	COOK: 35 MINUTES

INGREDIENTS

1 pound elbow macaroni

Three 12-ounce cans evaporated milk

2 teaspoons black pepper

2 teaspoons garlic powder

1½ teaspoons onion powder

1 teaspoon smoked paprika

1 teaspoon salt

2 cups shredded extra-sharp cheddar

1 cup shredded aged yellow cheddar

1 cup shredded aged white cheddar

1 cup shredded mozzarella

1½ cups shredded Colby Jack

Shoutout to my OG! As everyone knows, mac and cheese is not a dish you just decide to make one day and then get to be in charge of at the family gatherings. It takes practice, precision, and confidence! I took lots of notes from my grandmother, and with this recipe perfected, I believe the torch can finally be passed down to me.

1   Preheat the oven to 375°F. Bring a large pot of water to a boil. Add the macaroni and cook until al dente, 8 to 10 minutes. Drain and set aside.

2   In a large pot, combine the evaporated milk, black pepper, garlic powder, onion powder, paprika, and salt. Bring to a simmer low heat until the mixture has warmed completely, about 5 minutes.

3   Add the extra-sharp cheddar, yellow cheddar, and white cheddar. Mix well and simmer until the sauce thickens, 3 to 5 minutes. Remove from the heat.

4   In a large baking dish, layer one-third of the macaroni, one-third of the mozzarella, and one-third of the cheese sauce repeatedly until no more ingredients remain. Top with the Colby Jack.

5   Bake for 20 to 30 minutes, until golden brown (see Pro Tip).

Pro Tip

If you prefer a looser dish, dig in immediately. Otherwise, allow the mac and cheese to settle for 10 to 15 minutes after removing from the oven.

APPLE-BACON BRUSSELS SPROUTS

4 SERVINGS	PREP: 20 MINUTES	COOK: 30 MINUTES

INGREDIENTS

3 strips thick-cut bacon

½ teaspoon black pepper, divided

½ teaspoon garlic powder, divided

½ teaspoon onion powder, divided

1 pound Brussels sprouts,
  trimmed and halved

½ cup balsamic vinegar

2 tablespoons brown sugar

½ Granny Smith apple, diced

About two years ago, I had Brussels sprouts for the first time ever. From that point on, I never turned back. *However*, they have to be cooked right. If they don't have any kind of char, I don't want 'em! The different textures take these Brussels sprouts to the next level. If you've never been a fan, give 'em a try. Don't be scared—trust me!

1   Preheat the oven to 400°F.

2   Place the bacon on a baking sheet and cook in the oven for 10 to 15 minutes, until crispy. Remove the bacon from the baking sheet, leaving the bacon grease. Roughly chop the bacon.

3   Lightly season the pan with ¼ teaspoon each of the black pepper, garlic powder, and onion powder. Place the Brussels sprouts directly onto the pan and season with the remaining black pepper, garlic powder, and onion powder. Bake for 30 to 40 minutes, until crispy.

4   Meanwhile, combine the balsamic vinegar and sugar in a small saucepan.

5   Bring to a simmer until the mixture reduces to a glaze, about 10 minutes (see Pro Tip). Remove from the heat.

6   Transfer the Brussels sprouts to a large bowl and toss gently with the apple and bacon bits. Drizzle with balsamic glaze.

Pro Tip

Add in a few splashes of water if the sauce gets too thick.

SOUTHERN-STYLE FRIED CABBAGE
WITH SAUSAGE, BACON & PEPPERS

5 SERVINGS	PREP: 15 MINUTES	COOK: 30 MINUTES

INGREDIENTS

3 strips bacon

6 ounces turkey sausage (1 large link), sliced into rounds

½ small red bell pepper, sliced

½ small yellow bell pepper, sliced

½ small yellow onion, sliced

1 small to medium head of cabbage, sliced

1½ teaspoons sugar

1 teaspoon Cajun seasoning

1 teaspoon garlic powder

½ teaspoon black pepper

½ teaspoon smoked paprika

In my opinion, there aren't many vegetable dishes that are good completely on their own, but this is an exception. Another great way to make this dish is to put everything in small foil packets and wrap them up. Bake in the oven and you have a similar end result.

1   To a large pan over medium heat, add the bacon and cook until crispy, about 10 minutes. Transfer the bacon to a plate and crumble, leaving the grease in the pan.

2   Add the sausage to the pan and cook until slightly crispy and fully cooked, 2 to 3 minutes on each side. Transfer to the plate with the bacon.

3   To the same pan, add the bell peppers and onion. Cook until slightly tender, about 3 minutes.

4   Add the cabbage and fry, stirring occasionally, until wilted, about 3 minutes.

5   Add the sugar, Cajun seasoning, garlic powder, black pepper, and paprika. Toss well and fry until well incorporated, 1 to 2 minutes.

6   Add the bacon and sausage to the pan, then remove from the heat. Toss to combine. Enjoy!

HONEY JALAPEÑO CORNBREAD

5 TO 6 SERVINGS	PREP: 20 MINUTES	COOK: 30 MINUTES

INGREDIENTS

Baking spray

1 cup all-purpose flour

1 cup yellow cornmeal

1 cup sugar

1 tablespoon baking powder

¼ teaspoon salt

1 cup milk

2 large eggs

4 tablespoons butter, melted

1 to 2 small jalapeños, diced
   (see Pro Tip)

¼ cup honey

Everyone has had traditional buttermilk cornbread, or honey glazed, or blueberry...the list goes on! But this honey jalapeño cornbread will set your expectations of good cornbread even higher. If you're not a huge fan of spicy food, don't worry: The jalapeño is only a slight heat addition, and the honey cuts through the spice so well.

1 Preheat the oven to 350°F. Grease a medium cast-iron skillet or 9-inch square baking dish with baking spray.

2 In a medium bowl, combine the flour, cornmeal, sugar, baking powder, and salt.

3 In another medium bowl, whisk together the milk, eggs, and butter.

4 Slowly add the dry ingredients to the wet ingredients, stirring to form a smooth batter. Fold in the jalapeños.

5 Transfer the mixture to the skillet and smooth the top.

6 Bake for about 20 minutes or until a fork inserted into the center comes out clean.

7 Immediately drizzle with honey. Enjoy while warm!

Pro Tip

For a spicier cornbread, leave the jalapeño seeds in. For a milder version, remove the seeds before slicing.

CRISPY SMASHED GARLIC POTATO BITES

4 TO 5 SERVINGS	PREP: 12 MINUTES	COOK: 35 MINUTES

INGREDIENTS

1½ pounds small potatoes (such as Boomer Gold)

2 tablespoon olive oil

1 teaspoon salt

¼ to ½ cup grated Parmesan

3 tablespoons unsalted melted butter

Leaves from 2 rosemary sprigs, chopped

Leaves from 3 to 4 thyme sprigs, chopped

3 teaspoons garlic powder

1 teaspoon black pepper

1 teaspoon smoked paprika

These are my twist on French fries. I take small baby potatoes, toss them in oil and spices, and smash them to create an entirely new way to enjoy potatoes. Texture is very important here; make sure you cook these just right to ensure a crispy outer layer with a soft and fluffy inside!

1 Preheat the oven to 400°F.

2 In a large bowl, combine the potatoes, olive oil, and salt. Toss thoroughly, then transfer to a baking sheet. Bake for 20 to 30 minutes, until fork-tender. Transfer back to the bowl.

3 In another bowl, mix the Parmesan, butter, rosemary, thyme, garlic powder, black pepper, and paprika. Pour the mixture into the bowl with the potatoes (see Pro Tip).

4 Transfer back to the baking sheet and use a small glass to flatten each potato.

5 Bake at 400°F for another 5 to 10 minutes, until crispy.

Pro Tip

Save some of the butter mixture on the side and pour after the potatoes are crispy for extra flavor! (Some can be lost in the final baking process.)

CREAMED STEAKHOUSE SPINACH

6 TO 8 SERVINGS	PREP: 10 MINUTES	COOK: 30 MINUTES

INGREDIENTS

4 tablespoons unsalted butter

½ small yellow onion, finely diced

1 garlic clove, minced

2 tablespoons all-purpose flour

1½ cups heavy cream

¼ cup sour cream

4 ounces cream cheese

3 cups chopped cooked spinach (or 4 to 5 cups of frozen spinach, thawed and drained)

1 tablespoon garlic powder

1 teaspoon black pepper

1 teaspoon onion powder

1 teaspoon smoked paprika

½ teaspoon red pepper flakes

½ teaspoon salt

1 teaspoon lemon juice

¼ cup shredded mozzarella

Meals at traditional steakhouses are either going to have you thinking *this is delicious!* or *I could've made this ten times better at home for one third of the price.* But for me, creamed spinach is always the best part about eating at steakhouses. So if you love creamed spinach like I do, I got us covered. Enjoy!

1   Preheat the oven to 375°F.

2   Heat the butter in a medium pan over medium heat. Add the onion and garlic and cook until fragrant, 3 to 4 minutes.

3   Whisk in the flour to create a roux. Add the heavy cream, sour cream, and cream cheese and stir to combine. Reduce the heat to low.

4   Add the spinach, garlic powder, black pepper, onion powder, paprika, red pepper flakes, salt, and lemon juice. Mix well.

5   Stir in the mozzarella until melted and fully incorporated. Taste and adjust the seasoning if needed.

6   Bake for about 15 minutes, until bubbly and golden brown.

RED BEANS & RICE
WITH SAUSAGE

4 TO 5 SERVINGS	PREP: 15 MINUTES, PLUS 8 HOURS SOAKING TIME	COOK: 90 MINUTES

INGREDIENTS

16 ounces dried red beans

2 tablespoons vegetable oil, divided

14 ounces smoked turkey sausage, sliced

3 celery stalks, diced

½ small yellow onion, diced

½ small green bell pepper, diced

4 to 6 cups chicken broth (see Pro Tip 1)

2 teaspoons paprika

1½ teaspoons dried oregano

1 teaspoon garlic powder

1 teaspoon onion powder

½ teaspoon black pepper

3 bay leaves

Cooked white rice

Chopped fresh parsley

If you've never had red beans and rice before, let me warn you that you just might become addicted to it. When you cook this dish, the house will smell amazing, and you will be eager to dig in every minute you wait for it to be finished. Make this with Honey Jalapeño Cornbread (page 175) and thank me later.

1 Add the beans to a bowl and pour in just enough water to cover. Soak overnight or for at least 8 hours, then drain.

2 To a large pot over medium heat, add 1 tablespoon of oil and the sausage. Cook until seared, 2 to 3 minutes on each side, then remove from the pot.

3 To the same pot, add 1 tablespoon of oil, your celery, onion, and bell pepper. Cook until tender, 4 to 5 minutes.

4 Add the chicken broth, paprika, oregano, garlic powder, onion powder, black pepper, and beans. Mix, then add the bay leaves.

5 Bring to a boil, cover, and cook until the beans are tender, 45 minutes to 1 hour. (Uncover and stir the beans about every 10 to 15 minutes.)

6 Use a wooden spoon to crush some of the beans against the side of the pot (see Pro Tip 2). Reduce the heat to low and allow the beans to thicken, 20 to 30 minutes.

7 Stir in the sausage, then taste the beans and adjust the seasoning if desired.

8 Serve with rice and garnish with fresh parsley. Enjoy!

Pro Tips

1 Reserve extra chicken broth (or water) in case the beans begin to dry out in the cooking process. Add an extra ½ cup at a time while cooking if needed.

2 This will help thicken the broth. But don't smash all of the beans!

ARROZ CON GANDULES
(RICE & BEANS)

6 TO 8 SERVINGS	PREP: 15 MINUTES	COOK: 35 MINUTES

INGREDIENTS

1 tablespoon olive oil

¼ small green bell pepper, diced

¼ small yellow onion, diced

1 tablespoon recaito

1 to 1½ teaspoons black pepper

1½ teaspoons sazón

1 teaspoon adobo seasoning

1 teaspoon garlic powder

1 teaspoon onion powder

1 garlic clove, minced

One 15-ounce can pigeon peas

2 cups long-grain white rice, rinsed and drained

1 tablespoon chopped fresh cilantro

"Zo, what did you eat two to three times a week growing up?" **This. Dish. Right. Here. And I say that happily! This dish pairs with literally anything you can think of. When I was growing up, my grandmother would always make me a pot of this whenever I was hungry, and I was** *always* **asking her to make me something to eat. Throw in some chicken and you have an entire meal!**

1 To a medium pot over medium heat, add the olive oil. Stir in the bell pepper, onion, recaito, black pepper, sazón, adobo seasoning, garlic powder, onion powder, and garlic.

2 Add the peas and their canning liquid, then stir in the rice and cilantro. Add just enough water to cover the rice by ½ inch.

3 Bring to a boil, then reduce the heat to low and cover. Simmer until the rice is tender and the liquid is absorbed, about 20 to 25 minutes (see Pro Tip 1).

4 Remove the lid and fluff the rice with a fork (see Pro Tip 2). Enjoy!

Pro Tips

1 This is an old school tip! If the rice is too mushy after cooking, place a plastic shopping bag over the pot, place the lid back on top, and allow the rice to steam. This will absorb some of the moisture.

2 You may end up with a thin layer of burnt rice on the bottom of your pot. This is completely normal, and it's delicious!

SWEET POTATO MASH

5 TO 6 SERVINGS	PREP: 10 MINUTES	COOK: 95 MINUTES

INGREDIENTS

4 medium sweet potatoes, peeled and cut into chunks

¼ cup brown sugar

¼ cup granulated sugar

4 tablespoons unsalted butter, melted, plus more for serving

¼ cup maple syrup (optional)

1 teaspoon ground cinnamon

1 teaspoon vanilla extract

¼ teaspoon ground nutmeg

⅛ teaspoon ground cloves

This is one of my family's original Thanksgiving specials. Instead of a traditional garlic mashed potato or even baked yams, we would mash up sweet potatoes and create a delicious sweet potato mash. If you love sweet potato pie, this is pretty much a sweet potato pie without the crust. So you can imagine how this tastes!

1 Preheat the oven to 400°F.

2 Place the potatoes onto a sheet pan and bake for 60 to 75 minutes, until fork tender. Allow to cool, then peel and place into a large bowl.

3 In a small pot, combine the brown sugar, granulated sugar, butter, maple syrup if using, cinnamon, vanilla, nutmeg, and cloves. Bring to a low simmer until everything is completely warm, stirring constantly, until well incorporated, 4 to 5 minutes.

4 Slowly add the mixture into the sweet potatoes while mashing, until semi-smooth.

5 Top with more butter before serving if desired, and enjoy!

SWEET TREATS

Why is it that after every delicious meal, we always need something sweet? It's literally the icing on the cake of a good day. After a good meal, having something sweet makes an already perfect occasion ten times better! And of course, we can't forget the late-night sweet tooth.

Growing up, I was always sneaking into the kitchen late at night, trying to grab some dessert. Sometimes my Pops would fall asleep watching TV on the couch, and you had to be extra quick or he would catch you in the act. Good times, good times!

You can easily combine different desserts together and end up with an entire new concoction! My Peach Cobbler Pound Cake (page 207) is a great example of this. Peach cobbler and moist pound cake—who knew two desserts in completely different lanes could come together and be so good together? Whether you're a dessert fan or not, sometimes sharing something sweet with family or friends is just an extra excuse to spend time together. Now go make some delicious sweets and worry about that diet you were supposed to start later!

MOM'S FAMOUS SWEET POTATO PIE

ONE 9-INCH PIE	PREP: 20 MINUTES	COOK: 2 HOURS

INGREDIENTS

2 medium sweet potatoes

8 tablespoons unsalted butter, at room temperature

2 large eggs

1 teaspoon vanilla extract

½ cup packed brown sugar

½ cup granulated sugar

½ teaspoon ground cinnamon

½ teaspoon ground nutmeg

½ teaspoon salt

¼ teaspoon ground ginger

½ cup evaporated milk

1 tablespoon all-purpose flour

One 9-inch deep-dish pie crust

The best pie ever. No exaggeration in that statement, either. I've had a lot of pie in my life—pecan, cherry, apple—you name it. But nothing will ever beat a good slice of sweet potato pie after a delicious meal or in the middle of the night when that sweet tooth hits you. Shoutout to my mom for always making separate pies for everyone during the holidays!

1   Preheat the oven to 400°F.

2   Poke holes in the sweet potatoes, wrap them in foil and bake for about 1 hour until tender. Slice open and allow to cool completely.

3   Reduce the oven temperature to 350°F.

4   In a large bowl, mix the sweet potatoes, butter, eggs, and vanilla. Blend very well with a hand mixer.

5   Slowly incorporate the brown sugar, granulated sugar, cinnamon, nutmeg, salt, and ginger. Add the evaporated milk and blend thoroughly to form a silky batter.

6   Mix in the flour, then pour the batter into the pie crust. (The batter should be very loose!)

7   Bake for 1 hour, until the edges are golden brown and the pie is set in the center. Let cool for up to 3 hours.

LEMON MERINGUE PIE

| ONE 9-INCH PIE | PREP: 25 MINUTES | COOK: 20 MINUTES |

INGREDIENTS

Lemon Filling

One 9-inch deep-dish pie crust

1 cup sugar

3½ tablespoons cornstarch

2 tablespoons all-purpose flour

Pinch of salt

Zest and juice of 2 large lemons

2 tablespoons butter, softened

4 large egg yolks

Meringue Topping

4 large egg whites

4 to 5 tablespoons sugar

If you love lemon, this recipe is for you! This pie screams summer, warm weather, blue skies, and good vibes. Before some of you get frustrated making the meringue topping, you cannot have a drop of egg yolk in with the egg whites. Trust me, I ran through plenty of eggs in my cooking journey not realizing this! Let me save you some frustration.

1   Preheat the oven to 350°F. Prebake the pie crust for 5 to 10 minutes, until the edges are slightly brown.

2   **Make the filling:** To a medium pot, add the sugar, cornstarch, flour, and salt. Place the pot over medium heat and add 1 cup of water, the lemon zest, and lemon juice. Whisk slowly until it comes to a low simmer. Add your butter and whisk until fully incorporated.

3   Transfer about ½ cup of the mixture to a bowl with the egg yolks to temper. Whisking constantly, add the mixture back into the pot. Continue stirring over medium heat until the filling is thick, 5 to 10 minutes. Pour the filling into the pie crust.

4   **Make the topping:** Place the egg whites in a medium bowl. Beat or whisk thoroughly with a hand mixer until they become foamy. Slowly add in the sugar, about a tablespoon at a time, until you begin to see stiff peaks (see Pro Tip).

5   Spread the topping over the filling, creating a sort of dome over the pie.

6   Bake for 10 to 12 minutes, until the meringue is light brown on top. Let cool and enjoy!

Pro Tip

When the egg whites start to look like whipped cream, the meringue is nearly ready.

STRAWBERRY CINNAMON ROLLS

8 ROLLS	PREP: 45 MINUTES, PLUS 1 HOUR RISING TIME	COOK: 30 MINUTES

INGREDIENTS

Dough

1 cup milk, warmed

8 tablespoons butter, melted

2 large eggs, at room temperature

½ cup granulated sugar

2½ teaspoons instant dry yeast

1¼ teaspoons salt

4 cups all-purpose flour

Filling

1 cup packed brown sugar

8 tablespoons butter, softened

1 tablespoon ground cinnamon

1 teaspoon vanilla extract

¼ teaspoon ground nutmeg

Icing

2 tablespoons strawberry preserves

1 cup powdered sugar

¼ cup heavy cream

½ teaspoon vanilla extract

Baking spray

Cooking string

Cinnamon rolls hold a special place in my heart; they're the perfect balance of sweetness, cinnamon, and doughy bread. Since these are one of my favorite desserts, I had to figure out how to make them at home instead of buying them from the store. With a slight strawberry twist, these will definitely satisfy that sweet tooth!

1   **Make the dough:** In a large bowl, combine the milk, butter, eggs, granulated sugar, yeast, and salt.

2   Mix thoroughly, then gradually add in the flour. Continue mixing until a dough ball forms (see Pro Tip 1). Spray a large bowl with baking spray, then place the dough into the bowl and cover with a towel. Let rise for at least 1 hour at room temperature.

3   **Make the filling:** Meanwhile, combine the brown sugar, butter, cinnamon, vanilla, and nutmeg. Set aside.

4   **Make the icing:** To a small bowl, add the strawberry preserves, powdered sugar, heavy cream, and vanilla. Mix thoroughly. (See Pro Tip 2.)

5   Preheat the oven to 375°F. Spray a baking sheet or cast-iron skillet with baking spray.

6   Roll your dough out into a large square about ½-inch thick and evenly spread on the filling. Roll the dough tightly to form a log.

7   Use the cooking string or a knife to cut the dough into 1½-inch-thick rolls. Place them into the pan and bake for 20 to 25 minutes, until lightly browned.

8   Pour on the icing and enjoy while warm!

Pro Tips

1   If the dough gets a little sticky, add in a few pinches of flour.

2   For a warm glaze, microwave for 10 to 20 seconds before pouring it over the rolls.

SNICKERDOODLE COOKIES

24 TO 28 COOKIES	PREP: 30 MINUTES	COOK: 10 MINUTES

INGREDIENTS

2½ cups all-purpose flour

1½ teaspoons cream of tartar

¾ teaspoon baking soda

½ teaspoon salt

1 cup unsalted butter, softened

1½ cups sugar

2 eggs

1 teaspoon vanilla extract

½ teaspoon almond extract

Cinnamon Sugar

¼ cup sugar

1½ tablespoons ground cinnamon

¼ teaspoon ground nutmeg

Who knew something so simple could be so good? These soft, cinnamon-sugar-dusted cookies might just become your new Christmas cookies. Be careful with these; you may catch yourself eating a dozen before you realize it!

1   Preheat the oven to 350°F.

2   In a medium bowl, combine the flour, cream of tartar, baking soda, and salt.

3   In a large bowl, cream the butter and sugar for about 3 minutes. Add the eggs, vanilla, and almond extract. Mix thoroughly, scraping down the sides.

4   Adding a little at a time, mix the dry ingredients into the wet ingredients with a spoon. Set aside.

5   **Make the cinnamon sugar:** On a small plate, combine the sugar, cinnamon, and nutmeg.

6   Roll the cookie dough into 1½ tablespoon-sized balls. Roll the dough balls in the cinnamon sugar and place them onto a baking sheet.

7   Bake for about 10 minutes, until the cookies have risen and are lightly browned. For a crispier cookie, bake for 11 to 13 minutes. Remove from the oven and let cool completely. Enjoy!

SWEET HONEY BUN BARS

9 BARS	PREP: 25 MINUTES	COOK: 1 HOUR

INGREDIENTS

Baking spray

2 cup all-purpose flour

½ teaspoon baking soda

¼ teaspoon baking powder

⅛ teaspoon salt

8 tablespoons unsalted butter, softened

¾ cup granulated sugar

3 medium eggs, at room temperature

½ cup buttermilk

1 teaspoon vanilla extract

1 teaspoon almond extract

Cinnamon Sugar

⅓ cup packed dark brown sugar

2 teaspoons ground cinnamon

¼ teaspoon ground nutmeg

Glaze

½ cup powdered sugar

1½ to 2 tablespoons heavy cream

1 tablespoon maple syrup

½ teaspoon vanilla extract

When I was growing up, nothing was better than a heavily glazed honey bun from the corner store. My best friend Brian would literally sit at the store for a good 5 to 10 minutes, comparing which honey bun had the most glaze on it. Reminiscing on those days, I decided to create a dessert that gives you the flavor of a honey bun in a new way.

1 Preheat the oven to 325°F. Spray a 9-inch square baking dish with baking spray.

2 **Make the cinnamon sugar:** In a small bowl, combine the brown sugar, cinnamon, and nutmeg.

3 **Make the batter:** In a medium bowl, mix the flour, baking soda, baking powder, and salt.

4 In a large bowl, mix the butter and granulated sugar with a hand mixer until smooth and creamy. Slowly add in the eggs, mixing until fully incorporated, 1 to 2 minutes. Add the buttermilk, then stir in the vanilla and almond extracts.

5 Incorporate the dry mixture into the wet mixture slowly ensuring everything is well incorporated.

6 Pour half of the batter into the baking dish, add half of the cinnamon sugar, and then the remaining batter.

7 Take a knife and lightly swirl the batter. Bake for about 1 hour, until the bars are slightly golden brown. Remove from the oven, then sprinkle the remaining cinnamon sugar on top.

8 **Make the glaze:** Meanwhile, mix the powdered sugar, heavy cream, maple syrup, and vanilla in a small bowl. Brush it on top of the warm bars after baking.

9 Allow the bars to cool completely before slicing. Enjoy!

STRAWBERRY CREAM CHEESE DONUT HOLES

15 TO 20 DONUT HOLES	PREP: 20 MINUTES	COOK: 20 MINUTES

INGREDIENTS

1 cup strawberries, finely diced

1 cup sugar, divided

¼ cup lemon juice

1 teaspoon vanilla extract

2 teaspoons cornstarch

5 to 6 ounces cream cheese, softened

Neutral oil, for frying

One 16.3-ounce can biscuit dough

Quick question: What is the best type of donut of all time? Got your answer? Let's say it together on 3: 1…2…3…jelly filled! I hope that was your answer, too, because in my opinion, nothing beats it. This dish is a twist on a classic jelly-filled donut—an easy and fun recipe to recreate at home!

1   To a small pot over medium heat, add the strawberries, ½ cup sugar, lemon juice, and vanilla. Bring to a low simmer, 4 to 5 minutes, breaking up the strawberries with a wooden spoon.

2   In a small bowl, combine the cornstarch and 2 teaspoons of water to make a slurry. Add the slurry to the pot with the berries and remove from the heat. The mixture should thicken up.

3   Place the cream cheese into a small bowl, then strain the strawberry mixture through a small mesh strainer into the bowl. Mix thoroughly and set aside. Let cool completely.

4   Preheat 2 to 3 cups of frying oil in a medium sized pot to 375°F.

5   Cut the biscuit dough into 2-inch pieces. Roll the dough into balls and drop them into the frying oil to fry until golden brown, 3 to 4 minutes, flipping halfway through.

6   Immediately remove the donuts from the oil and toss them in the remaining ½ cup sugar.

7   Fill an injector with the strawberry filling and inject the filling into the donut holes (see Pro Tip). Enjoy!

Pro Tip

If you can't find an injector, place the filling into a small sandwich bag and cut one of the bottom corners off. Cut a hole into each donut and fill them that way!

GRANDMA'S OATMEAL RAISIN COOKIES

12 TO 15 COOKIES	PREP: 20 MINUTES, PLUS 1 HOUR CHILL TIME	COOK: 10 MINUTES

INGREDIENTS

1¼ cups margarine, softened

¼ cup granulated sugar

¾ cup packed dark brown sugar

1 large egg

1 teaspoon vanilla extract

½ teaspoon almond extract

1½ cups all-purpose flour

1 teaspoon baking soda

½ teaspoon salt

3 cups old fashioned oats

½ cup raisins

Baking spray

There's just something about oatmeal raisin cookies that touches my soul. Some people love chocolate chip, others love peanut butter, but oatmeal raisin will forever be my #1. If you don't like raisins, I don't have anything else to say except that you're missing out! My grandmother would make bags on top of bags of these cookies and give them to us as "Christmas gifts"—and we would all gladly accept them every time. Thank you, Ma!

1   In a large bowl, combine the margarine and granulated sugar. Mix until smooth, then add the brown sugar and mix again until smooth.

2   Add the egg, vanilla, and almond extract. Mix well, scraping down the sides of the bowl.

3   In a medium bowl, combine the flour, baking soda, and salt. Slowly add this mixture to the wet ingredients and mix well until no dry spots remain.

4   Fold in the oats and raisins and mix thoroughly to incorporate. Allow the dough to sit in the refrigerator for at least 1 hour.

5   Preheat the oven to 375°F. Spray a baking sheet lightly with baking spray.

6   Drop 2 tablespoon-sized dough balls onto the sheet, leaving space between each dough ball.

7   Bake for 10 to 12 minutes, until the cookies have flattened, then remove from the oven and let cool (see Pro Tip). Enjoy while warm.

Pro Tip

The cookies may not look like they are done when you remove them from the oven, but they will continue to cook slightly while cooling.

BLUEBERRY TOASTER STRUDELS

4 TO 6 SERVINGS	PREP: 30 MINUTES	COOK: 35 MINUTES

INGREDIENTS

1½ pounds blueberries
(fresh or frozen)

½ cup granulated sugar

Zest and juice of 1 lemon

1½ teaspoons vanilla extract

2 tablespoons cornstarch

3 to 4 sheets premade pie crust
dough, cut into rectangles
(see Pro Tip 1)

Neutral oil, for frying

Glaze

1 cup powdered sugar

¼ cup heavy cream

We all remember those delicious toaster strudels we ate growing up, right? They came with a small pack of icing for each strudel. Well, I obviously had to recreate them for us adults! Make a bunch of these, freeze them, and cook them whenever your heart desires. Perfect for breakfast or dessert!

1   To a small pot over medium heat, add the blueberries, sugar, lemon zest, lemon juice, and vanilla.

2   Cook, breaking up about half of the blueberries, to form a sauce, 5 to 10 minutes.

3   In a small bowl, mix the cornstarch and 3 tablespoons of water to make a slurry. Add the slurry to the pot and cook until thickened, about 5 minutes. Remove from the heat and let cool completely.

4   Spoon about 2 teaspoons of blueberry filling onto the center of a pie crust rectangle.

5   Place another pie crust rectangle on top of the filling and crimp every side closed with a fork.

6   Repeat steps 4 and 5 with the remaining dough and filling (see Pro Tip 2).

7   Place the pastries in the refrigerator for about 10 minutes to cool.

8   **Make the glaze:** In a small bowl, combine the powdered sugar and heavy cream. Microwave for about 30 seconds.

9   Fill a medium pot three-fourths of the way with oil and heat to 375°F.

10 Fry the pastries until lightly golden brown, 2 to 3 minutes. Top immediately with the glaze and enjoy!

Pro Tips

1   Cut the pie crusts into even rectangles—a traditional premade rolled pie dough should yield 4 to 6 rectangles

2   If you have leftover filling, use it to top pancakes for a delicious syrup alternative!

WHITE CHOCOLATE S'MORES DIP

4 TO 6 SERVINGS	PREP: 10 MINUTES	COOK: 5 MINUTES

INGREDIENTS

10 to 12 graham crackers, broken into pieces

Two 4-ounce white chocolate bars, broken into pieces

½ cup salted caramel sauce

1½ cups mini marshmallows

Chocolate syrup

It's hard to beat classic s'mores, with marshmallows toasted over an open fire. But if you don't have access to an open fire, I promise this dip will make you forget all about those classic s'mores. It's a very simple and fun recipe to make. Perfect for the kids!

1 Preheat the oven to 350°F.

2 Cover the bottom of a cast-iron skillet with one layer of the graham crackers. Cover with the chocolate pieces.

3 Drizzle on the salted caramel, then top with marshmallows. Crush up a few of the graham crackers and sprinkle them on top.

4 Bake for about 5 minutes, until the chocolate is melted and the marshmallows are light brown. Drizzle with chocolate syrup. Enjoy!

PEACH COBBLER POUND CAKE

ONE 10-INCH POUND CAKE	PREP: 45 MINUTES	COOK: 90 MINUTES

INGREDIENTS

Baking spray

3 cups all-purpose flour,
plus more for dusting

1½ cups butter or margarine,
at room temperature

3 cups granulated sugar

6 jumbo eggs, at room temperature

1 teaspoon vanilla extract

½ teaspoon almond extract

Peach Sauce

Three 15-ounce cans peaches
in heavy syrup

½ cup packed brown sugar

¼ cup maple syrup

1 tablespoon ground cinnamon

1 teaspoon cornstarch

½ teaspoon ground nutmeg

Glaze

1 cup powdered sugar

3 tablespoons heavy cream

The cake of all cakes, the star of the show, the heavy hitter—whatever you want to call it, this cake is a winner! Imagine a moist pound cake, mixed with a delicious peach cobbler. What a beautiful creation! If you're in charge of bringing a dessert to a family gathering, trust in me and this will be the star of the dessert table.

1   Preheat the oven to 325°F. Spray a 10-inch pound cake or angel food cake pan with baking spray, then liberally dust with flour.

2   To a large bowl, add the butter. Cream with a hand mixer, then slowly add in the granulated sugar and mix on medium until the mixture resembles fluffy mashed potatoes, about 1 minute.

3   Slowly mix in 1 egg at a time, gradually adding more flour in between eggs, until completely incorporated. Make sure to scrape down the sides. The batter should be thick and smooth. Add the vanilla and almond extracts.

4   Pour the batter into the pan and spread the top evenly.

5   Bake for 80 to 90 minutes, until a crust forms and a toothpick inserted into multiple areas comes out dry. Let cool.

6   **Make the peach sauce:** Drain two of the cans of peaches, then add all of the peaches to a small pot over medium-low heat. Add the brown sugar, maple syrup, cinnamon, cornstarch, and nutmeg. Cook until the mixture begins to thicken, 6 to 8 minutes, then turn off the heat and let cool.

7   **Make the glaze:** In a small bowl, mix the powdered sugar and 1 tablespoon of heavy cream at a time until thick and smooth.

8   To assemble, remove the cooled cake from the pan. Drizzle on the glaze, then add the peaches on top. Pour the remaining syrup from the peach mixture into the center of the cake. Enjoy!

NO-BAKE BANANA PUDDING CHEESECAKE

ONE 9-INCH CAKE	PREP: 30 MINUTES, PLUS 7 HOURS CHILL TIME	COOK: 8 MINUTES

INGREDIENTS

Crust
Baking spray

1½ cups graham cracker crust

8 tablespoons unsalted butter, melted

¼ cup sugar

Filling
36 ounces whipped cream cheese

1½ cups sugar

Juice of ½ lemon

1 teaspoon vanilla extract

2 tablespoons instant banana cream pudding mix

25 to 30 vanilla wafers

2 small bananas, peeled and sliced

Salted caramel sauce

Cheesecake can be intimidating, but this no-bake cheesecake is easier to make than you think. Banana pudding is one of the greatest desserts ever, so fuse it into a cheesecake and you create a masterpiece. But if you don't love bananas, don't worry—the banana flavor in this cake is very subtle. This is a dessert everyone can enjoy!

1 Preheat the oven to 350°F. Lightly coat the bottom of a 9-inch springform pan with baking spray.

2 **Make the crust:** Add the graham cracker crust to a small bowl. Stir in the butter and sugar until the mixture becomes thick and coarse. Press the mixture into the bottom of the pan and about half of the way up the sides.

3 Bake for 7 to 8 minutes, until the crust has begun to harden and hold together. Remove from the oven and let cool completely for 2 hours in the refrigerator.

4 **Make the filling:** In a medium bowl, using a hand mixer or whisk, mix the cream cheese, sugar, lemon juice, and vanilla. Stir in the pudding mix until smooth.

5 Reserve about ¼ cup of filling, then pour the remaining filling into the crust and smooth out the top.

6 Let sit in the refrigerator for at least 5 hours (12 hours is ideal). Remove the cake from the pan and place the vanilla wafers around the side of the crust, using small amounts of the reserved filling to help them stick. Top with sliced bananas, crushed and whole vanilla wafers, and a drizzle of caramel sauce.

7 Chill the cake in the refrigerator for at least 30 minutes to an hour, until the consistency is similar to a thick pudding. Slice and enjoy!

RED VELVET CHEESECAKE BROWNIES

9 BROWNIES	PREP: 25 MINUTES, PLUS 1 HOUR COOLING TIME	COOK: 30 MINUTES

INGREDIENTS

Brownies

Baking spray

1 cup granulated sugar

2 large eggs

½ cup unsalted butter, melted

¼ cup cocoa powder

1 tablespoon red food coloring

1 teaspoon vanilla extract

1 teaspoon white vinegar

¼ teaspoon almond extract

Dash of salt

¾ cup all-purpose flour

Cheesecake

6 ounces cream cheese, at room temperature

¼ cup granulated sugar

1 large egg, room temperature

1 tablespoon lemon juice

1 teaspoon vanilla extract

Stay with me, y'all. We took three different desserts here and combined them into one. If you love red velvet cake, cheesecake, and brownies, imagine them together! Perfectly moist brownies, creamy cheesecake, and the red velvet flavor just pops. Double up the recipe—they may be gone quickly!

1   Preheat the oven to 350°F. Spray an 8-inch square baking pan with baking spray.

2   **Make the brownies:** In a large bowl, combine the sugar, eggs, butter, cocoa powder, food coloring, vanilla, vinegar, almond extract, and salt until smooth.

3   Slowly fold in the flour until well incorporated, but be careful not to overmix.

4   **Make the cheesecake:** In a small bowl, mix the cream cheese, granulated sugar, egg, lemon juice, and vanilla.

5   Pour the brownie batter into the pan. Drop clumps of cheesecake batter on top and gently swirl the top with a knife.

6   Bake for 30 to 45 minutes, until a toothpick inserted into the center comes out smooth (see Pro Tip). Let cool at room temperature for 1 to 2 hours.

Pro Tip

If you prefer a chewier consistency, bake for another 10 to 15 minutes.

SIGNATURE DRINKS

This is one of my favorite parts of the book!
I love getting creative and coming up with different food recipes, but developing drink recipes is a ton of fun. Just a little of this, a lot of that, and you end up with the perfect concoction!

Everyone knows there's nothing better than a cold glass of something after a delicious meal, or a strong glass of something after a long day. Is it just me or do ALL of my drinks need to be cold? The idea of a lukewarm drink after finishing a meal just rubs me the wrong way. The only exception is a perfect mug of hot chocolate on a freezing day. Any other time, pass me the ice! Drinks are best enjoyed cold, and you can't convince me otherwise.

If you love a good cocktail, you have to try the Eatwitzo Special (page 233). It's so simple, yet delicious! I mean, the name is already special, so it has to be good. Am I right or am I right? If you love a good treat, definitely give the Cookie Butter Milkshake (page 218) a try. Perfect for kids (or big kids a.k.a adults!) if you make it nonalcoholic, it's a twist on a cookies and cream shake that just might become your new favorite.

WHITE HOT COCOA

2 TO 3 SERVINGS	PREP: 10 MINUTES	COOK: 12 MINUTES

INGREDIENTS

¼ cup cocoa powder

¼ cup brown sugar

¼ cup granulated sugar

2 cups whole or 2 percent milk

1 cup heavy cream

1 teaspoon vanilla extract

½ cup chopped white chocolate

Mini marshmallows

Whipped cream

Chocolate shavings

This drink brings back memories of playing in the snow with my brothers, our hands and feet freezing cold. We would drop our outside clothes at the door and have a warm cup of hot chocolate—it was the dream. Whether it's winter or summer, this hot cocoa is perfect for getting under a blanket, turning on a good movie, and just enjoying the moment!

1   In a medium pot over low heat, warm the cocoa powder, brown sugar, and granulated sugar, stirring to incorporate, 2 to 3 minutes.

2   Add the milk, heavy cream, and vanilla. Cook until small bubbles begin to form and the mixture has reached a very low simmer, 3 to 4 minutes.

3   Add the white chocolate and stir constantly until all of the chocolate has melted and the mixture has become thick and creamy, 2 to 3 minutes.

4   Pour into mugs and top with marshmallows or whipped cream. Garnish with chocolate shavings and enjoy!

CLASSIC SOUTHERN SWEET TEA & LEMONADE

5 TO 6 SERVINGS	PREP: 15 MINUTES	COOK: 15 MINUTES

INGREDIENTS

5 black tea bags

1 to 2 cups sugar (see Pro Tip)

1 cup lemon juice
  (from 5 to 6 large lemons)

Ice

Lemon slices

Fresh mint sprigs

When I was growing up, we always had big family reunions every other year. Lots of fun, memories, and good food. One of the most important things my great-grandmother would make was a pitcher of sweet tea and a pitcher of lemonade. While I'm not a huge fan of sweet tea by itself, mixing it together with lemonade is a moment I'll never forget. A glass of this over ice on a hot summer day? Amazing!

1   **Make the tea:** To a medium pot, add 4 cups of water and bring to a boil.

2   Place the tea bags in a large bowl or pitcher and pour the hot water onto the tea bags. Steep for up to 10 minutes. Remove and discard the tea bags.

3   **Make the lemonade:** To a small pot over low heat, add the sugar and 2 cups of water. Heat until the sugar has completely dissolved, creating a simple syrup.

4   In a pitcher, mix the lemon juice with 1 cup of water. Mix in the tea and simple syrup, then transfer to the refrigerator to cool completely.

5   Serve over a tall glass of ice on a hot day. Garnish with lemon slices and fresh mint and enjoy!

Pro Tip

Use 1 cup of sugar for a less-sweet drink and up to 2 cups for a sweeter drink.

COOKIE BUTTER MILKSHAKE

1 SERVING	PREP: 12 MINUTES

INGREDIENTS

4 Biscoff cookies

3 to 4 scoops vanilla ice cream

¼ cup whole or 2 percent milk

2 tablespoons Biscoff cookie butter, plus more for the rim

1 ounce RumChata (optional)

Whipped cream

Caramel syrup

Growing up, I spent summers in Florida—long pool days, great dinners, and making milkshakes by hand late at night. For some reason, a milkshake always tastes better when you whip it in a cup by hand. I definitely used this method before I was old enough to use the blender. Same end result, same great taste!

1. Crush the cookies, reserving one for garnish. Place the crushed cookies onto a plate.

2. In a blender, combine the ice cream, milk, cookie butter, and RumChata, if using. Blend well.

3. Spread the cookie butter around the rim of your glass, then roll it in the crushed cookies.

4. Pour the milkshake into the glass and top with whipped cream.

5. Garnish with the reserved cookie by sticking it into the glass and drizzle with caramel syrup. Enjoy!

COQUITO

INGREDIENTS

13.5 ounces cream of coconut

14 ounces sweetened condensed milk

12 ounces evaporated milk

1 teaspoon vanilla extract

½ teaspoon ground cinnamon

¼ teaspoon ground cloves

¼ teaspoon ground nutmeg

1 cup cognac, such as Hennessy,
   plus more to taste (optional)

3 to 4 cinnamon sticks

Ice

Can't have the holidays without coquito! It's one of my Pops's specialties. When my brothers and I were growing up, and before we were old enough to drink the alcoholic version, my father would always make a container of coquito for us to enjoy. One time, he had us help him make it—and out of nowhere, the top of the blender came off, creating a mess in the entire kitchen. Cleanup crew was in full effect that day!

1   To a blender, add the cream of coconut, condensed milk, and evaporated milk. Blend until smooth.

2   Add the vanilla, cinnamon, cloves, and nutmeg and blend again.

3   Add the cognac, if using, blend again, and taste. Add more cognac if desired (see Pro Tip).

4   Place 2 to 3 cinnamon sticks into large mason jars and pour in your coquito.

5   Allow to chill in the refrigerator for 4 to 8 hours. Shake well and serve over ice with a fresh cinnamon stick to garnish.

Pro Tip

If the drink is too strong, dilute it with equal parts sweetened condensed milk and coconut cream.

HOLIDAY PARTY PUNCH

6 SERVINGS   PREP: 10 MINUTES PLUS 1 HOUR CHILL TIME

INGREDIENTS

2 cups cranberry juice
2 cups orange juice
1 cup pineapple juice
1 cup vodka (optional)
1 orange, thinly sliced
1 lemon, thinly sliced
1 cup ginger ale
Rosemary sprigs
Whole cranberries (optional)
Ice

Something delicious to sip on throughout any holiday gathering! This punch is so refreshing, and it can be made with or without the alcohol. Grab a bunch of plastic cups (or glasses, if you're feeling fancy) get your family together, and enjoy a good time!

1 In a large pitcher, mix the cranberry, orange, and pineapple juices.

2 Add the vodka, if using. Mix again, then transfer to the refrigerator for at least 1 hour.

3 Add the orange and lemon slices to the pitcher.

4 Top with the ginger ale and garnish with rosemary and cranberries, if using. Pour over ice and enjoy!

FROZEN STRAWBERRY-PEACH BELLINI

4 TO 5 SERVINGS   PREP: 10 MINUTES

INGREDIENTS

2 cups frozen peach slices

1 cup frozen strawberries

1 cup ice

2½ to 3 ounces simple syrup

Juice of 1 lemon

3 cups champagne or sparkling wine

Mint leaves (optional)

Fresh strawberries

I'll never forget traveling out to Houston in the summer and seeing how popular frozen drinks were. At almost every restaurant I went to, I grabbed a frozen drink—partially just because they were delicious, and partially because it was so hot. Whip up a couple of these on a hot day, and let yourself relax.

1   In a blender, combine the frozen peaches, frozen strawberries, and ice. Blend until smooth.

2   Add the syrup and lemon juice, then give it another quick blend to incorporate the flavors.

3   Add the champagne and blend in 10-second increments until fully incorporated.

4   Pour into a glass and garnish with mint, if using, and fresh strawberries. Enjoy!

STRAWBERRY HENNESSY LEMONADE

INGREDIENTS

Ice

2 to 3 lemon slices

1 strawberry

4 ounces lemonade

1 ounce Hennessy

1 ounce strawberry syrup
cocktail mixer

Strawberry and lemonade is an undefeated combination. It's good almost everywhere you go, the perfect balance of sweet and sour. Now imagine it spiked with a little cognac, poured over cold ice, and you have the perfect date-night drink! Make a few appetizers, turn on some music, and enjoy the night.

1   Fill a glass with ice. Add the lemon slices. Cut a slit into the strawberry and add to the rim.

2   In a cocktail shaker, combine the lemonade, Hennessy, and strawberry syrup.

3   Add a few ice cubes and shake well until fully incorporated and chilled.

4   Slowly pour the cocktail into the glass.

Pro Tip

If you like a stronger drink, feel free to add another shot of Hennessy.

WATERMELON LEMON DROP

1 SERVING	PREP: 7 MINUTES

INGREDIENTS

¼ cup cubed watermelon

2 ounces vodka

½ to 1 ounce triple sec

Juice of ½ lemon

½ ounce simple syrup

Ice

Sugar

Chilled cocktail glass

Lemon slices

Watermelon slices

My fiancée is a lemon drop connoisseur. Not only are they refreshing, but they also can pack quite the punch—if you know what I mean! Add in the watermelon and this drink turns into a refreshing summertime experience! If you can find good-tasting watermelon outside of the summertime, let me know so I can get some, too!

1   To a cocktail shaker, add the watermelon and muddle thoroughly, breaking up the pieces finely to get all of the watermelon flavor out.

2   Add the vodka, triple sec, lemon juice, and simple syrup.

3   Add a few ice cubes, then top the shaker and shake well for 15 to 30 seconds.

4   Pour some sugar onto a plate. Rub the rim of your glass with lemon, then dip it into the sugar.

5   Pour the cocktail into the glass. Garnish with fresh lemon and watermelon and enjoy!

ORANGE CRUSH CHILLER

INGREDIENTS

2 ounces orange-flavored vodka

Juice of 1 small orange

1 ounce heavy cream

½ ounce triple sec

Chilled cocktail glass

Crushed ice

Splash of club soda

Orange slices

Imagine an orange Creamsicle transformed into a drink! One of the factors that really enhances this drink is crushed ice. While it isn't a requirement, it can sometimes make or break a drink. Sip one of these, close your eyes, and you might feel like you're at the beach!

1   In a cocktail shaker, combine the vodka, orange juice, heavy cream, and triple sec. Mix thoroughly for at least 30 seconds.

2   Fill your glass with crushed ice. Pour in your cocktail mixture.

3   Top with club soda and garnish with an orange slice. Enjoy on a hot day!

EATWITZO SPECIAL
(RUM & LEMONADE)

| 1 SERVING | PREP: 5 MINUTES |

INGREDIENTS

Ice

3 ounces dark rum, such as Bumbu

½ cup lemonade

¼ cup club soda

Lemon slice

Mint leaves

My ultimate go-to after a long day, to celebrate, or to enjoy a good time. This drink is light (or heavy, if you down a few of them) but downright delicious. So if you ever create this cocktail at home, think of me nd make an extra one, because I promise I'd toast the glass if I were there with you!

1   Fill a glass with ice.

2   Pour in the rum, then add the lemonade. Fill to the rim with club soda.

3   Garnish with lemon and mint, and enjoy!

SAUCES

The thing that can make or break a dish, the thing that we cover our wings in and dip our fries in, the thing that can bring the best out of a meal: SAUCE!

There are so many types of sauce, so there's no denying that there are a few staples that need to be in your rotation. But can we agree on one thing real quick: Is it just me or is ranch arguably the best condiment of all time? It is so versatile and tastes good on so many things, I don't think I can live without it. So I had to make my own version: Easy Buttermilk Ranch (page 239). Have fun using these sauces in recipes throughout the book!

HOMEMADE ALFREDO SAUCE

| 2 CUPS | PREP: 10 MINUTES | COOK: 12 MINUTES |

INGREDIENTS

2 tablespoons butter

4 garlic cloves, minced

2 cups heavy cream

1½ teaspoons black pepper

1½ teaspoons onion powder

1½ teaspoons dried oregano or
Italian seasoning

1 teaspoon garlic powder

½ teaspoon smoked paprika

½ teaspoon salt

¾ cup grated Parmesan

Chopped fresh parsley (optional)

Now we all love a good Alfredo pasta, but it's time to put the jarred Alfredo sauces back on the shelves! After making this recipe, I want you all to really see how easy it is to make fresh, delicious Alfredo sauce. Spice it up, add whatever you want—this is the perfect base recipe.

1   Melt the butter in a medium saucepan over medium heat.

2   Add the garlic and cook until fragrant, about 1 minute.

3   Slowly add the heavy cream, stirring constantly. Stir in the pepper, onion powder, oregano, garlic powder, paprika, and salt. Cook until the sauce reaches a low simmer and begins to bubble, 3 to 5 minutes.

4   Reduce the heat to low. Slowly add the Parmesan, stirring until the sauce has thickened and can coat the back of a spoon, about 3 to 4 minutes. Remove from the heat, sprinkle on some parsley, and enjoy!

Pro Tip

If the sauce is too watery, simmer on low until thickened to your desired consistency. If the sauce is too thick, slowly add in tablespoons of heavy cream until the sauce has thinned out.

EASY BUTTERMILK RANCH

2 TO 3 CUPS

PREP: 5 MINUTES, PLUS 2 HOURS CHILL TIME

INGREDIENTS

1 cup mayonnaise

1 cup sour cream

½ to 1 cup buttermilk (see Pro Tip)

Juice of ½ small lemon

1 tablespoon garlic paste

1 tablespoon dried dill

1 tablespoon fresh parsley

2 teaspoons black pepper

2 teaspoons chili powder

2 teaspoons onion powder

Greatest condiment ever? Ranch goes well with almost anything. While it can be a little intimidating if you've never made it before, you will probably always make your own from this point on. Double up the recipe, store it in a mason jar in the fridge, and use it on everything!

1   In a large bowl, mix the mayonnaise and sour cream until no lumps remain. Stir in the buttermilk and lemon juice until smooth.

2   Add the garlic paste, dill, parsley, black pepper, chili powder, and onion powder. Mix thoroughly, taste, and adjust the seasoning if needed.

3   Tightly wrap the bowl with plastic wrap, transfer to the refrigerator, and allow to cool for up to 2 hours.

Pro Tip

The amount of buttermilk you add will change the consistency of the final product after cooling. If you prefer a thinner ranch, add more buttermilk. If you prefer a thicker ranch (great for dips!), add less.

BBQ SAUCE

| 2 CUPS | PREP: 7 MINUTES | COOK: 8 MINUTES |

INGREDIENTS

1 cup ketchup

¾ cup brown sugar

¼ cup apple cider vinegar

1½ tablespoons Worcestershire sauce

⅓ cup honey

½ teaspoon coarse black pepper

½ teaspoon cayenne

½ teaspoon garlic powder

½ teaspoon chili powder

½ teaspoon onion powder

½ teaspoon liquid smoke (optional)

When I make this sauce, I can smell the smoke from the grills, feel the 80-degree weather, hear some good music playing, and feel a cold drink in my hand. This is a simple staple barbecue sauce recipe that will suit all of your summer grilling needs! Make it spicy with some cayenne and use as a dipper for anything you desire.

1   To a small pot over medium-low heat, add the ketchup, brown sugar, vinegar, and Worcestershire sauce. Cook, stirring occasionally, until everything is well incorporated, 2 to 3 minutes.

2   Add the honey, black pepper, cayenne, garlic powder, chili powder, onion powder, and liquid smoke, if using.

3   Continue stirring until the sauce is smooth, 3 to 4 minutes. Remove from the heat and let cool.

4   Enjoy as a glaze or dipping sauce!

HOMEMADE TOMATO SAUCE

ABOUT 5 CUPS	PREP: 12 MINUTES	COOK: 75 MINUTES

INGREDIENTS

1½ teaspoons olive oil

½ small onion, diced

½ small green bell pepper, diced

5 garlic cloves, minced

3 ounces tomato paste

Two 28-ounce cans crushed tomatoes

1 tablespoon dried oregano

2½ teaspoons black pepper

2 teaspoons garlic powder

2 teaspoons salt

2 tablespoons sugar

There is nothing like a classic tomato sauce. This one is cooked slowly, allowing all of the flavors to break down and marinate together—it's a necessity! Having had a lot of spaghetti and tomato sauce growing up, I had to try my hand at creating a recipe from scratch. I think I did pretty well, if I do say so myself!

1   Heat the olive oil in a large pot over medium heat. Add the onion, bell pepper, and garlic and cook until tender, about 5 minutes.

2   Stir in the tomato paste, then add the tomatoes, oregano, black pepper, garlic powder, and salt. Stir well, then lower the heat to a low simmer.

3   Simmer until the sauce has thickened slightly, at least 45 minutes. Every 15 minutes, add a few tablespoons of water, stirring occasionally you've added ½ cup. After 45 minutes, add the sugar.

4   Let simmer until the sauce is smooth and blended, another 15 minutes, then remove from the heat.

5   Use this recipe in any dish that calls for a red sauce or dip bread into it!

Pro Tip

If your sauce is too thick, add small amounts of water at a time, stirring and cooking on a low simmer until you reach your desired consistency.

INDEX

U

V

W–X–Y–Z

T

ACKNOWLEDGMENTS

We did it! Those who have stuck with me through the long journey of becoming who I am today and influencing this book, I thank you! My family, I thank you. My friends who are just like family, I thank you. My team who are just like family, I thank you. And to my supporters who are like family, I thank you!

This process was not easy, but we've finally made it to the finished product: an amazing book that is an accurate representation of who I am. I wouldn't be who I am today, and this book wouldn't be what it is without the help from and influence of everyone around me. The circle you put yourself into is truly an accurate representation of you, and I couldn't ask for a group of better people.

First and foremost, I would like to shout out my parents. Thank you Moms and Pops for raising me, always providing, and always believing in me. I promise I got y'all forever and hope to continue making you both proud!

Next, I have to give my fiancée (soon-to-be wife) Mia her shine. You are the person that sees all of the behind the scenes, the ups and downs, the late nights and early mornings. Thank you for continuously pushing me and being in my corner—I couldn't have done this without you.

To my babygirl Ava! Thank you for trying all of the sweet treats in this book— you made sure they were all good!

Now I can't forget about the person that keeps me on my toes, Lex! Thank you for helping me make all of this happen, keeping everything in order and making sure I'm taken care of. I look at you as family!

Big O! Olivia, thank you, thank you, thank you for making all of this possible. If it wasn't for you none of this would have been brought to life! You helped turn a dream into reality, and I am forever thankful.

The 700 Piedmont Avenue crew! The team! We killed it! Ashley, Jonathan, Will, and sous-chef Terence. I literally could not have finished this project without you four. We worked hard and got things done: "Look alive everyone!"

The extended team! The ones behind the scenes that I'm so thankful for: I truly appreciate you, Diamond, Lindsay, Mike, and Bill!

Last but certainly not least, a special thank you to all of my supporters. Each and every one of you holds a special place in my heart. You made all of this possible. I promise to always strive to deliver nothing but the best to you all. If I could go back and do everything over, I wouldn't change a thing. Now, let's get cooking!

WHO IS EATWITZO?

His name is Lorenzo Espada—some call him Zo or Renzo, but you can call him whichever you prefer! He's a 24-year-old guy from North Carolina who simply loves to cook. Of African American and Puerto Rican heritage, Zo has been heavily influenced by both cultures in developing his cooking style. When he was 21 and his daughter was born, he knew he had to finish school, figure out who he wanted to be in his life, and learn how to be a father at the same time. He always knew he wanted big things for himself; he didn't know how he would get there, but bringing her into the world pushed him to make sure it happened.

As a child, Zo used to dream of becoming an entrepreneur: making your own way, taking risks, and shooting for the stars. While the road is never easy, it's certainly always work out at the end of the day. Zo went through the motions of failure early on in his business to finally seeing success (making it through a pandemic!). Eventually, he began to grow, learn, and truly step into his purpose by bringing positivity and cooking together.

Now, he creates recipes, great meals, and opportunities for people to enjoy eating with their family and friends. The young boy who aspired to be a chef one day is now living out his dream. Find him @eatwitzo on social media.